THE

ORVIS®

— GUIDE TO —

BEGINNING FLY FISHING

THE
ORVIS®
— GUIDE TO —
BEGINNING FLY FISHING

101
TIPS for the
Absolute
Beginner

Illustrations by
BOB WHITE

Preface by
NICK LYONS

Tom Rosenbauer

SKYHORSE PUBLISHING

Copyright © 2009 by Tom Rosenbauer
Photographs © 2009 by Tom Rosenbauer
Illustrations © 2009 by Bob White

Skyhorse Publishing books may be purchased in bulk at special discounts for sales promotion, corporate gifts, fund-raising, or educational purposes. Special editions can also be created to specifications. For details, contact the Special Sales Department, Skyhorse Publishing, 307 West 36th Street, 11th Floor, New York, NY 10018 or info@skyhorsepublishing.com.

Skyhorse® and Skyhorse Publishing® are registered trademarks of Skyhorse Publishing, Inc.®, a Delaware corporation.

www.skyhorsepublishing.com

10 9 8 7 6 5 4 3

Library of Congress Cataloging-in-Publication Data
Rosenbauer, Tom.
The Orvis guide to beginning fly fishing : 101 tips for the absolute beginner / Tom Rosenbauer.
      p. cm.
ISBN 978-1-60239-323-3 (alk. paper)
1. Fly fishing. I. Orvis Company. II. Title.
SH456.R664 2008
799.12'4--dc22

                                    2008052281

Printed in China

*To **Bob Murphy** (1944–2009), who was always
the perfect hunting and fishing buddy: A patient
mentor, endless source of advice on everything from
steelhead fishing to dog training, and a true gentleman
who inspired everyone he ever met to be a better person.
I'll think of you whenever I'm on the water.*

Contents

Preface

IT LOOKS IMPOSSIBLE. AND CERTAINLY TOO COMPLICATED. But there is a moment in the life of the beginning fly fisher when he suddenly turns a corner. What seemed unintelligible now makes good sense. What seemed disconnected is marvelously all part of a coherent process. What was impossible—casting a fly beyond one's shoelaces, choosing a fly with even a faint chance of gulling a fish, "reading" the water, catching a trout or a bass or a pike or a bluefish—now is something one has done and something one can expect to do again many times.

Ah, it's not only possible, but great fun. There is a kind of electric shock when a fish strikes your fly, and a quiet satisfaction.

Fly fishing can indeed seem impossible. There seem to be a thousand occasions for error. Mostly, the people I've met who have tried and then not pursued fly fishing fall into a variety of different camps. Some find it too fussy; some are frustrated trying to learn the few basic casts. Some lose their first couple of fish because their knots didn't hold. Some like spinning or bait casting or trolling or catfish grabbing and don't know why they should change. Some are afraid to fail. Some try fly fishing and don't master it enough to find pleasure there. I felt many of these issues myself when, after a childhood fishing in other ways—quite successfully—I began to *not* catch fish with a fly rod.

I had no mentor, but I persisted. And when I finally got to doing it fairly well, and with decent success, I found that the further I practiced and the more time I spent on the water, the more proficient I became at it, the more inexhaustible its pleasures were. I have now fished far and near with immense pleasure. And I have become fascinated by how people learn and how they develop.

This nifty little book by Tom Rosenbauer will save the novice much of the discomfort I felt and will bring him—or her—to a position of some confidence. I have read previous books by Tom, and all reveal his special clarity and helpfulness. He is a superb fly fisher and an excellent, patient teacher.

What makes *The Orvis Guide to Beginning Fly Fishing* particularly valuable is that it is the distillation of many years of teaching novices and more advanced fly fishers what they need to know to fish better. Tom knows all of the questions most frequently asked, and he knows the most practical and helpful answers he has given.

The questions: answering these is the heart of this book.

Here are the central problems beginners have, the questions that have kept them from progressing at a decent rate. Clear, practical, genuinely helpful advice—that's what this book provides.

How I wish I'd had Tom's book when I had so many of the basic questions, when I knew so little I once threaded a fly line through the little keeper ring (used to hold the fly on the end of your line) and wondered why I couldn't cast.

This little book is chock-full of valuable answers and hints and tips—and it will quickly get you on the water, catching a variety of fish, enjoying yourself greatly.

Bravo, Tom!

—Nick Lyons
February 2009

Introduction

YOU WALK INTO A FLY SHOP, REVOLVE AROUND THE FLY bins for a few minutes, wander back to the wall full of gadgets, then finger the endless file of fly rods that all look the same. You've been told you need something called a tippet to go fly fishing, but don't have a clue what a tippet looks like, whether it attaches to the rod or the reel, or how much one costs. Meanwhile, the shop manager is deep in quiet discussion with a couple of weathered young guys who are probably guides, and although she looks friendly, you're afraid to ask such a basic question, so you leave unfulfilled and frustrated.

This is your book. In close to forty years of teaching fly fishing—in print, on the Web, in schools, and through podcasts—I've heard it all. I've also heard the same questions over and over through the years, and they really don't change much with each generation of new fly fishers. Fly fishing is easy in concept (you cast a tiny lure out there on a weighted line with a skinny leader, and a fish bites it) but we often get caught in the nuances. How quickly do I strike? How long should my fly stay on the water? How quickly do I gather line?

I've tried to pre-empt these common questions by setting them down in manageable bites that will answer your questions and get you jump-started quickly. There are many comprehensive books on fly fishing, but often you just need a quick answer and don't have time to read through a chapter or two to get it. I think you'll find many of your questions are answered here. I hope I've provided quick enough answers to get you going, and to encourage you to study the topic in more depth with other resources, including the list of essential books I've provided in the last chapter.

Fly fishing is popular and visible today. It's elegant, intellectual, and it takes you to the most beautiful places in the world. Looking at general-interest magazines and television commercials, you'd think every third person in North America is a fly fisher. Yet as far as we can determine, out of forty million anglers in the United States, only about five million are serious fly anglers. The attrition rate of this consuming sport is high because in order to do it well you have to do it often, and most people today don't think they have the time to fly fish often and thus never become proficient enough to feel comfortable. Part of the problem is that adults and children just don't have enough free time in their lives, but more specifically, people think they have to get on an airplane and fly to Montana or the Bahamas to have fun fly fishing.

In fact, most of us have a place to fish with a fly within five miles of our homes. Steelhead run rivers in the middle of Rochester and Chicago and Cleveland. Largemouth bass, tarpon, and exotic peacock bass lie ready to grab a bass bug in the canals around Miami. World-class carp fishing with a fly is found almost everywhere, even in downtown Denver and Los Angeles. I learn something new every time I go fly fishing, even though I've been doing this for so many years and live on the banks of a trout stream. You will, too, and the skills you develop while having fun catching eight-inch sunfish in Central Park will serve you well when you *do* find time to take that exotic trip.

—Tom Rosenbauer
February 2009

Getting Started

1

How do you get started if you don't have a mentor?

IN THE FIRST PART OF THE TWENTIETH CENTURY, FLY-fishing skills were passed from parents, patient relatives, or friends to novice fly fishers. A lucky find at a local library might turn up a ragged copy of Ray Bergman's *Trout*. But without the advantage of helpful videos, modern photographs, and clear illustrations, learning fly fishing without a mentor was an exercise in frustration. Today, you have rich sources of information, from hundreds of books and DVDs to free resources on the Internet. But when you need to ask, "What went wrong with my cast?" or "How should I present that dry fly?" these sources fall mute.

The best place to begin is at a fishing school. The emphasis in schools and clinics is on fly casting, which is the most difficult aspect of fly fishing to master, and whether you learn to cast from a school or on your own, make sure you're comfortable with the basics of casting before you go fishing. Most schools are run by people with proven skills at teaching fly fishing and you'll benefit from their experience at identifying quick ways to improve your fly casting. You can choose from independent schools, classes run by tackle companies, or free clinics held by local fly shops. But not everyone has the time or the inclination to learn in a classroom setting. To some they are a painful reminder of high-school algebra. Others are too anxious to get right on the water and enjoy the calming sunshine of a June morning in the middle of a river.

The next best option is a reliable and understanding fishing guide. Some guides are comfortable with novices and others have neither the temperament nor the patience to spend the day removing a client's flies from streamside brush. If you want to learn on a guide trip, explain to the guide that you are a rank beginner—do not overestimate your skills, as a guide can see through your deception after a few casts—and that you are interested as much in learning technique as you are in catching fish. If the guide seems reluctant on an initial phone call, make a polite exit and try a different guide. And pick your location carefully. Saltwater fishing for bonefish or tarpon, fishing for trout on rivers that are termed "technical," or steelhead fishing in the middle of winter are not places to learn. Fishing for trout in stocked or wilderness waters where the fish strike eagerly, chasing small striped bass or redfish in saltwater estuaries, or fishing for bass and panfish in lakes are experiences that will teach you important skills and still allow an expectation of a fish on the end of your line.

You may not want to pay for a guide or a fishing school because of economics or principle. Finding a mentor is difficult but not impossible these days. First, in any social situation, try to identify yourself as a beginning fly fisher. It's amazing how many fishing buddies have come together this way, and the bonding that can happen when two fly fishers realize a common passion in an otherwise boring or uncomfortable event is almost instantaneous.

Join a local Trout Unlimited, Coastal Conservation Association, or Federation of Fly Fishers chapter. These organizations often have a circle of members who take great pleasure in introducing new people to fly fishing,

Along the banks of a river, you can sometimes find friendly anglers willing to answer your questions, no matter how basic.

and if you show interest in volunteering for local stream improvement or cleanup projects you'll get acquainted quicker than you would by sitting in the back corner at monthly meetings.

The most unreliable but sometimes the most satisfying way to learn more about fly fishing is by finding an impromptu mentor on the banks of a trout stream or on a lonely beach at dawn. But you have to be careful about whom you ask for advice. Avoid groups of three or four people fishing close together—they are probably fishing pals taking a trip together and you may feel like the new kid in school trying to sit down at the lunch table with the football team. I would also avoid the lone angler with a tense, crouched posture staring intently at the water. This guy has just traveled for hours to do battle with a trout and does not want to be distracted with small talk.

Look for the lone angler standing on the bank with relaxed posture who seems to be in no hurry to get into the water. He's already been on the river for a week, or is retired and fishes there every day, and may be very generous with advice and helpful hints. Approach him slowly and away from the water so you don't spook any fish that may be close to the bank, offer a pleasant greeting, and read his tone of voice and body language. If he offers some advice, listen, and once he starts fishing, ask if you can watch what he does. Just stay on the bank and don't wade into his pool, as there is nothing that betrays your lack of knowledge more than crowding a fellow fly fisher.

2

The best way to practice your casting

THERE IS NO FLY-FISHING CIRCUMSTANCE WHERE CASTING poorly will offer an advantage. I recently hosted a week-long bonefishing trip to the Bahamas where one angler went fishless until the very last day. Despite being a good sport about it, I could sense his frustration welling up and I knew he was not having a good time. Although the weather was cooperative and not windy, he was still not able to place a fly with any accuracy because he had not taken the time to practice his casting before the trip. On his last morning on the islands, I woke him up at dawn and made him practice, without the distraction of feeding fish or the pressure of a guide watching over his shoulder, on the lawn in front of his hotel room. After an hour of practice he was placing his fly wherever he wanted at forty feet. That day he caught and released three bonefish, and when I caught up with him at the dock after fishing I was worried his smile would pop his jaw out of its socket.

You must feel comfortable with that fly rod in your hand before you spend time, money, and emotional capital on a fishing trip. And there is no substitute for practice. Find a place where you have fifty feet behind and in front of you, with perhaps twenty feet of clearance on each side. This can be your lawn, a park, a rooftop, parking lot, alley, or a deserted gym. Water is essential for practicing casts like the roll cast or

You can practice casting wherever you have enough room. No water required.

spey cast, but for the overhead cast, which you'll use 90 percent of the time, dry-land casting is fine. Try to practice when no one is around so you won't be distracted and won't have to answer platitudes about how many you've caught.

Use the same line you'll be fishing with. Most of the time this will be a floating line, but if you plan to use a sinking line, practice with one because you'll need to adjust your timing for the denser character of the line. Never cast without a leader. Fly lines are designed to be cast with a leader on the end, which slows the casting loop at the end and offers air resistance that adds the finishing touch to your cast. Finally, tie to the end a piece of brightly colored yarn that mimics the size and air resistance of the flies you'll be using. If you have old flies, cut the point off one and use that instead. Place an object thirty or forty feet away. Now work on your accuracy. The ability to hit a six-inch target at forty feet about 20 percent of the time means you're ready to go fishing, as long as the other 80 percent of your casts are not far off.

Avoid the temptation to cast the entire fly line. Few fish are caught at seventy feet, even in the ocean, and casting the whole line is like eating before you learn to chew. If you will be fishing in the ocean or a on very wide river, back up and stretch out your casts to fifty or sixty feet, but remember that accuracy still counts at that distance. If you can't hit the target, you are better off wading closer to the fish or asking your guide to move the boat closer.

Try to practice casting in the wind. The chances of fishing on a totally windless day are slim, so be prepared. Practice with the wind in your face, when you'll ease up on your back cast and put more speed into your forward cast. Then turn around and cast with the wind, which is not as easy as it sounds. Wind behind you pushes your back cast down, which can spoil your casting loops or fire a fly into your ear on the way forward. Then play with crosswinds. For a right-hander, a left-to-right wind is safe and easy because the wind pushes the fly away from you, and all you have to do is aim upwind to make your fly land on target. A right-to-left wind is another story for a right-hander. You should avoid this dangerous wind, which pushes line into your body, if possible. If you can't avoid a crosswind, practice casting across the front of your body or actually turn around and cast behind yourself, dumping your "back cast," then turn around to face your target after the line hits the water.

Don't kill yourself with practice. You are much better off casting thirty minutes a day for three days than spending an hour and a half in a single session, because once your arm gets tired the practice ends up being a work-out instead of a tune-up. Fly casting at this distance requires very little strength—it's almost all timing—so if your arm gets tired, you've been doing it too long or you are gripping the rod too hard. (In fact, a loose grip on the rod actually improves your casting because it dampens vibrations and smoothes out your cast.)

Casting practice is a chore, but you should resist the plan that you'll straighten out the kinks once you hit the water. Even world-champion casters practice regularly, and if you're not totally confident in your ability, a few hours of practice will exponentially increase the success of your next fishing trip.

3

The two knots you must be able to tie on the water

THERE ARE SCORES OF FLY-FISHING KNOTS, AND AT FIRST the number of knots you'll see can be confusing. Most of these can be done at home, with lots of light and plenty of time to practice; for instance, tying a nail knot to a fly line to attach a leader or tying an Albright knot to attach your backing can be done before a fishing trip. But once you're on the water, you will change flies or lose them, so you'll need to be practiced at tying a fly to the tippet. You'll also need to tie two pieces of tippet material together when lengthening your leader or adding a lighter piece of material if you choose to step down to a much smaller fly. For nearly every situation except fishing for big-game species like sailfish or tarpon, the only knots you'll need are a clinch knot and a surgeon's knot.

The clinch knot is used to tie two pieces of monofilament leader or tippet material together. It works with nylon or fluorocarbon equally well. If you've done any spin fishing or bait casting, you probably already know this knot. There is a variation of this knot called the improved clinch knot, but it's neither improved nor necessary—the basic one works just as well and is easier to tie and to tighten.

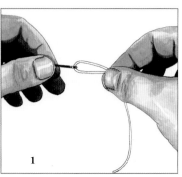

1

The surgeon's knot connects two pieces of monofilament. Like the clinch knot, it is equally strong with nylon or fluorocarbon, and it also works perfectly to connect these two unlike materials together. In contrast to the hard-to-tie barrel or blood knot, it works with materials of widely different diameters. For instance, whereas a barrel knot connecting 5X to 2X material (a difference of 0.003 inch) will break easily, a surgeon's knot connecting the same two materials will retain nearly 95 percent of the strength of the lighter material.

Clinch Knot

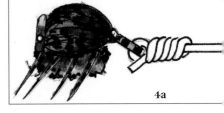

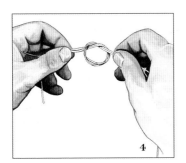

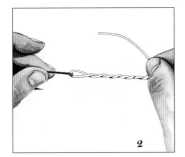

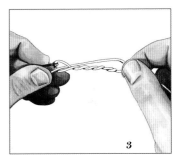

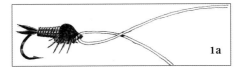

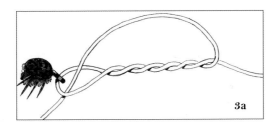

Surgeon's Knot

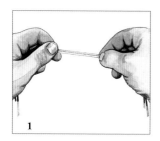

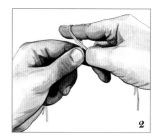

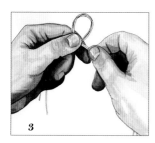

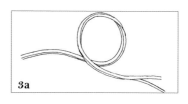

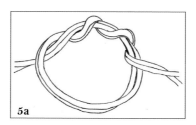

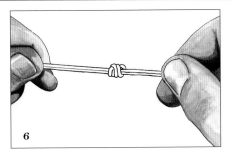

6

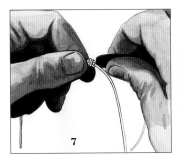

7

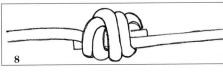

8

There are scores of knots that perform the same tasks as these two, but these are the ones I use on the water, and the only time they've failed me is when I forgot to wet my knots (a bit of saliva as lubricant helps them tighten firmly) or when I neglected to test a knot before presenting a fly to a fish.

4

Exactly how much fly-fishing gear do you need to get started in trout fishing?

A VERY COMMON AND NATURAL REACTION FROM PEOPLE who want to begin fly fishing is, "There is so much stuff! What do I need to just get started?" One of the allures of fly fishing is that it can be so complex and many people enjoy the accumulation of new gear. But it does not need to be that way. My advice is to start small and then just add to your tackle collection when you really find a need for something new.

Here's an example of how simple it can be. I live on a small trout stream. The other day when I got home from work, I realized my wife Robin had locked me out and I didn't have a house key. Now, I always keep a rod and reel rigged and ready to go, hanging on a couple of nails behind the house. Still in my street shoes and office clothing (granted, the Orvis dress code is pretty casual, but it's still not what I would consider fishing attire), I grabbed my rod and reel, with a small streamer fly already attached to the leader, and walked down to the river.

I have one pool on my property where I can cast without getting into the river. I made about three casts, hooked and released a ten-inch brown trout, and walked back to the house. It was pure luck. If I had lost that fly in the trees I would have been dead in the water (excuse the pun). If I needed to get into the water to get a better angle on a cast, I would have ruined my shoes—plus, the water was cold.

So here is bare minimum:

- A fly rod
- A floating fly line to cast the fly (you'll want a floating line 95 percent of the time for trout fishing)
- A fly reel to hold the line

You don't need a lot to go fly fishing—a rod, reel, line, leader, a box of flies, and maybe a pair of waders and a waist pack to carry a few things.

- A leader to present the fly, to smooth out the cast, and to keep the heavy fly line away from the fish
- A fly

Whether you fish a pond or a stream, eventually you'll want to get into the water. The fish might be farther than you can cast, or you might not get enough back cast room by standing on shore. In a lake the answer is a canoe, kayak, rowboat, or float tube. In a stream, the answer is a pair of waders, or at least a pair of wading shoes and shorts if the weather is warm enough.

What happens when you lose a fly, or the fish won't eat the one fly you have? You can carry a bunch of flies in a pocket, but I don't recommend it. You can be like the famous fishing writer Nick Lyons and carry extra flies in an old Sucrets tin. Or you can buy a fly box or two and keep your flies neat and secure.

Leaders break and get too short after a lot of fly changes, so you'll eventually want to replace the terminal end of your leader, known as the tippet. Smart anglers carry at least three different sizes of tippet material on spools because flies much larger or smaller than the one you're using now might require a different size tippet.

Some of us use our teeth to cut leader material, but as you get older the enamel wears away and you just can't get a nice clean, close cut with those old choppers. Plus, your dentist will wag his finger at you. So a pair of fisherman's snips will make your knots neater and save your teeth for corn on the cob after you retire.

If you fish with dry flies, unless you only use flies made from closed-cell foam, you'll need a silicone-based fly floatant to keep them floating. For releasing fish and for crimping the barbs down on flies, a pair of forceps helps. You can fish nymphs without a strike indicator and split shot, but you'll eventually want to get them.

About the only truly dangerous aspects of fly fishing are falling in a fast current and getting a hook stuck in your eye. Polarized glasses can ease your fears with both—they'll cut glare from the water and let you see submerged holes and rocks, and they'll keep an errant hook from sticking in the most vulnerable part of your anatomy (any other place is painful, but more embarrassing than anything else). A hat also protects your head from hooks and keeps glare out of your eyes. Your standard baseball cap works as well as anything.

You can keep all this stuff in a pocket, but eventually you'll either need to buy a shirt with lots of pockets or wear something else to carry your gear. The traditional garb is a fishing vest with pockets, but the popularity of fishing vests is being challenged by new lightweight chest packs.

So to the very basic list mentioned earlier you'll probably want to add:
- Waders
- Wading shoes
- A fly box or two full of basic trout flies

- A few spools of tippet material
- Fly fisherman's snips
- Fly floatant
- Split shot
- Strike indicators
- Forceps
- Polarized sunglasses and a hat
- Vest

Of course, as you progress in fly fishing you'll discover lots of other neat gadgets for making your time on the water more fun, but with the gear listed above I could happily fish all year. At least in my backyard.

5

What to get after the essentials

ALTHOUGH YOU CAN FISH WITH JUST THE BASIC STUFF FOR the rest of your life, eventually you'll discover some gadgets and gear to make your time on the water easier and more fun. Some anglers decry the proliferation of gadgets that can hang from a fishing vest, but others enjoy trying new widgets and feel they're part of the allure of fly fishing. Just don't rush into the acquisition of gear too quickly. Wait until you've got a few trips under your belt. Keep a mental or written list of problems you have, and then look for solutions in your local fly shop, tackle catalog, or hardware store.

Here are some suggestions of things that aren't essential, but that I find to be truly useful on the water:

- A rain jacket. If you primarily fish in waders, get one of the "shorty" styles that won't hang in the water when you are wading. If you fish from a boat or from shore, you can get away with a longer style.
- Fingerless or thin neoprene gloves for cold-weather fishing, and thin sun gloves for tropical and high-mountain fishing in warm weather. Skin cancer is a real threat to fly fishers, and gloves are as essential as a hat if you're sensitive to ultraviolet rays.
- Knot tying tools. If you have trouble with knots, many clever tools have been invented to make knot tying easier.
- A diamond file for sharpening hooks. It's a lot more convenient and economical to sharpen a hook than to throw away a three-dollar fly.
- A net. Fish are easier to land, photograph, and release with a net. You can land many fish with your hands, but you'll lose more at the final moment. The amount of time spent battling with a fish will be cut in half when you carry a net.
- A net retainer with a quick-release mechanism to keep the net out of the way until you need it.

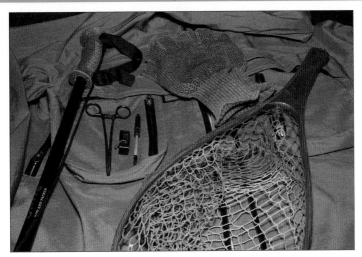

After you acquire the essential gadgets, think about a rain jacket, wading stuff, a few tools, a net, and a pair of fingerless gloves if you plan to fish in cold weather.

- A wading staff if you fish big rivers. Having a third leg makes a big difference. Many wading staffs collapse and stay out of the way until you need them.
- Sunscreen and insect repellent. Why be miserable?

6

Planning your first fishing trip

I WOULD NOT SPEND A LOT OF TIME OR MONEY ON YOUR very first fly-fishing trip. You'll make mistakes, you'll realize your casting limitations, and you'll have plenty of questions that you may have to research after your trip. It doesn't make sense to waste a week of your valuable time and thousands of dollars for a trip to New Zealand, or even a day of time and a hundred miles on your car, when you can find a place for your first trip much closer to home.

My first suggestion would be to find the closest pond or lake. There are few ponds in the lower forty-eight states that don't have a population of sunfish or other panfish. These feisty little guys strike eagerly, they aren't spooky, and fly selection is not critical as long as you fish a fly that's small

A patient guide will help you enjoy your first big fly-fishing trip.

enough to fit into their diminutive mouths. They also tend to hang close to shore so you won't have to worry about long casts or dealing with waders or a boat. You'll fine-tune your casting and will learn how to strike fish, how to strip in line to bring them to hand, and how to release them. Don't forget to bring a pair of forceps, as these fish often swallow a fly with such abandon that it gets lodged beyond where you can reach with your fingers. If the pond has small largemouth or smallmouth bass, so much the better. They are slightly harder to catch, but bass under ten inches are more eager than their adult relatives.

You can also find panfish or large minnows like fallfish and creek chubs in streams close to home. These streams may be ignored by most anglers because they don't have any trout or other gamefish, but you're just out there to practice—and besides, it helps if you don't have to worry about who is watching your technique. In addition, the current in these streams will teach you about manipulating your fly in moving water, something that most of us forget about when practicing in the backyard or on casting ponds.

7

What to do when you first get to the water

A LITTLE OBSERVATION BEFORE YOU ENTER THE WATER and begin casting will make your fishing day more productive and fun. Whether you're launching a boat or wading a river, take a few minutes to observe the water before disturbing it with your presence. The best fish in a body of water are not necessarily a half mile upstream or on the other side of the lake—fish take the best habitat for feeding, regardless of how close it is to an access point, and you might frighten some nice fish by making premature waves.

Try to observe the water from a high vantage point if possible, which gives you a better look into the water than you would have at the water level. I often climb a hill above the water before fishing, even if it means getting out of breath for a few minutes, because it helps to slow me down and also alerts me to deep pockets or submerged objects in the middle of the river that might harbor nice fish, stuff I would never see if I just waded into the water. Once you've scoped the water for inanimate objects, look for fish.

Look for subtle dimples of trout taking tiny insects, wakes in the shallows from cruising redfish, or smallmouth bass crashing minnows in the shallows. Next, look for prey. Are there baitfish in the water? What size and shape are they? Are there insects on the surface or in spiderwebs along the bank? A few minutes of careful study may help you pick the best fly of the day.

For the sake of others and for your own fishing success, look for other anglers. Disturbing another angler might spoil someone else's day and even evoke harsh words, and following another person in a river or on a lake forces you to fish water another angler has already fished, water that is probably already disturbed and devoid of feeding fish.

Although few anglers carry them, a small pair of binoculars can greatly enhance your initial surveillance. Is that a big log out in the middle of the river or a twenty-inch brown trout? Are those insects mayflies or caddisflies? Is that shape along the bank that's just out of sight a dead tree or another fly fisher waiting for the hatch?

Usually, the best way to start a day on the water is to sit and quietly observe the water, looking for feeding fish or likely fish-holding spots.

8

Fly fishing in urban areas

YOU MAY FEEL SELF-CONSCIOUS FISHING CLOSE TO A sidewalk or along a busy highway, subject to long stares and smarmy comments from pedestrians, but some of the best fishing you have might be right under your nose. I've caught steelhead in downtown Rochester, New York, and Grand Rapids, Michigan. I've stalked carp in sight of the Denver skyline and on a golf course in Houston. You can catch striped bass within the city limits of San Francisco and New York, peacock and largemouth bass (plus tarpon and bonefish!) in Miami, and trout in the suburbs of Atlanta.

Because boat traffic and swimmers disturb cautious gamefish, the best time to fish urban areas is from dawn until the first rays of sunlight hit the water, which probably fits in best with your work schedule, anyway. Multiple-piece rods and a minimum of tackle also allow you to commute by car or bicycle or train with your tackle right after fishing, and if you wear waders, a pair of wrinkle-free pants lets you arrive in the office with no one the wiser.

I don't know of a single urban area in North America that does not have fly-fishing opportunities within the city limits. It might not be as peaceful and prestigious as the Florida Keys or wilderness trout, but that doesn't mean the fishing is any less appealing or challenging. The more you fish with a fly the better you'll get, and fishing close to home a few days a week, even if it's bluegills in Central Park, will sharpen your skills for that summer trip to Alaska. There is not a better way to start your day, and I guarantee you'll forget about the noise and bustle around you in short order.

You don't have to travel to the wilderness to catch fish on a fly. This hefty lake trout was caught on a fly in the middle of Grand Rapids, Michigan.

Equipment

9

Pick a rod by line size

THE FIRST DECISION ABOUT PICKING A FLY ROD HAS nothing to do with your height, weight, strength, location, or casting skill. The physical weight of a fly rod is also insignificant. The first thing to decide is what line size you need. Every fly rod made is designed for a specific line size (although some may handle several with some adjustment in casting style). These sizes are based on the weight in grains of the first thirty feet of the line, regardless of whether the line floats or sinks, because it's the weight of the line bending the rod that lets you cast. Luckily, you and I don't need to memorize these grain weights because all fly-fishing manufacturers use a number system that ranges from 1 through 15, where each line size correlates to a grain weight. It's used by every maker of fly rods throughout the world.

The smaller the number, the lighter the line. Lighter lines, in sizes 1 through 4, deliver a fly with more delicacy. They cast small flies and light leaders best, but don't cast as far as heavier lines and don't handle the wind as well. As lines get heavier, in the 5 through 7 range, they lose some delicacy but gain in their ability to deliver larger flies and longer casts, and you won't have to fight the wind as much. These middle sizes are most often used for trout and smallmouth bass. Sizes 8 through 10 are considered the basic rods for long casts, big flies, and lots of wind, and are the sizes most often used by saltwater, bass, and salmon anglers. But they splash down heavier and won't protect a light tippet as well as the lighter rods. When you get into line sizes 11 and heavier, you're really looking at a rod designed to fight big fish, because once you get to a 10-weight rod, you've probably maximized the distance you'll get and going heavier only gives you more power to turn the head of a big tarpon or shark.

Fortunately, the flexibility of the rod needed to throw each line size corresponds perfectly with its purpose. Rods designed for lighter fly lines are very flexible, so it's easier to play a trout on a two-pound tippet with a flexible 4-weight rod. If you fish a leader with a two-pound tippet on a 9-weight rod, you'll most likely break most fish off on the strike because the stiffer rod is not as good a shock absorber, and besides, fishing a heavy 9-weight line on top of spooky trout will send most fish running for cover before they even see your fly. Playing a small trout on a 9-weight rod is not much fun, anyway, because the rod will hardly bend against the wiggles of a ten-inch fish. And playing a ten-pound redfish on a 4-weight might be fun for a few moments, but the lighter rod just does not have the strength to land a big fish sounding under a boat, something a stiffer rod will do with ease.

Just by looking at this small stream with clear water you can expect that a 4-weight line would be about perfect.

10

How long should your rod be?

I ONCE ASKED A TOURNAMENT CASTER IF THERE WAS AN optimum rod length for casting, ignoring all the other tasks we ask of a fly rod. Without hesitating, he answered "eight and a half feet." The physics of fly fishing are not easily understood, and air resistance, line weight, loop shape, and line speed all come into play, so I won't begin to theorize as to why eight and a half feet is the optimum length. But if all you ever wanted to do was cast out in the open with no wind, and had no conflicting currents to worry about, you'd want an eight-and-a-half-foot rod.

But fishing is much more than casting. In small, brushy places, an eight-and-a-half-foot rod gets tangled in the brush as you walk from one spot to another, and the wider casting arc of a longer rod offers overhanging trees more chances to snatch your fly and leader. A rod that is between six and seven and a half feet long is better for brushy streams, with the really short ones best for almost impenetrable woodland brooks, while rocky mountain streams with wider banks, where if you can get midstream you have plenty of room in front of and behind you, allow rods up to eight feet long before they get clumsy.

Rods longer than eight and a half feet are best for bigger waters. It's easier to keep your back cast off the ground behind you with a longer rod, they are better at making casts over fifty feet, and when you need to mend line or hold line off the water to prevent drag, that extra six inches make a surprising difference. Nine-foot rods seem to be the perfect length for saltwater fly fishing and give a great balance between making longer casts and the ability to play a large fish. It's actually easier to play large fish on a shorter rod as opposed to a longer rod, though, and that is why 14- and 15-weight rods for huge sailfish, marlin, and tuna are usually made in eight-and-a-half-foot lengths. They don't cast as well as nine-footers, but these species are typically teased close to the boat with a hook-less plug or bait so casts longer than fifty feet aren't needed.

To manipulate a fly line over these tricky currents, a fly rod nine feet long or longer would be the most efficient tool.

Really long rods, ten feet and over, are best when tricky currents require the angler to manipulate the fly line once it hits the water. Because the swing of a fly is so important in salmon and steelhead fishing, and these fish are often caught in very wide rivers, two-handed rods up to fifteen feet long are sometimes used with special casts called spey casts that can pick up sixty or seventy feet of line and deliver it back on target without false casting and without the line ever going behind the angler.

11

How to pick a reel

FOR FISH LIKE SMALL TROUT, PANFISH, AND BASS, A FLY REEL
is simply a line storage device. It keeps your line neat and orderly when you
walk to and from fishing, and also keeps excess line from tangling at your
feet and around the clutter that fishing boats seem to attract. Nearly all of
the reels you see are single action, which means that one revolution of the
handle moves the spool around once. Unlike spin fishing or bait casting,
where you retrieve line after each cast and a multiplying action comes in
handy, it's not needed in fly fishing. In the past, automatic reels with spring-
loaded spools and multiplying reels with gear systems were made, but these
reels proved to be heavy and clumsy, not to mention difficult to maintain in
good working order.

Smaller reels don't need strong drag tension, either. All that's needed is
enough tension on the reel to prevent the line from back-lashing on the

A narrow arbor trout reel on the left compared to the heavier, large arbor
saltwater reel on the right.

spool when you pull some off, and perhaps some light tension if a bass or trout pulls a few feet of line when fighting. This tension might be provided by a simple click mechanism composed of a spring and a small metal triangle called a pawl, that engages teeth on the reel spool, or it can be from a small disc drag system. The main considerations when looking for a small reel are how nice it looks and how much it weighs, as the more expensive reels are lighter and more attractive than the less expensive entry-level reels.

Many fish run a hundred yards or more when first hooked. Big trout, salmon, steelhead, and most saltwater species will yank from five feet to a hundred yards of line during a battle, and it's difficult to put tension on a reel by grabbing the fly line with your fingers, as it is neither precise nor uniform, and grabbing a fly line when a fish is running usually leads to a broken leader. These fish require a mechanical, adjustable break system or drag to help you tire them; otherwise they'll just swim away until they steal all your line and backing. Fly reels for these species employ a disc drag system like the brakes on your car, and these drags are most often made with a cork or plastic disc against the aluminum frame of the spool. These bigger reels also require extra capacity for the one hundred to four hundred yards of backing you'll need. Thus, when looking for a reel for these species, check the capacity to make sure it will hold the line size you have plus the maximum length of backing you'll need.

In big-game fishing for tarpon, marlin, sailfish, or tuna, where the fish run as fast as a car and may keep up the pace for hundreds of yards, drag strength is critical, as is the ability of the reel's design to dissipate the heat generated by the friction of the drag surfaces. In the middle of a battle with a marlin, lesser fly reels get so hot they smoke and then seize up completely. There is no way for a consumer to tell if a fly reel is up to this challenge, and the only way to assure yourself of a reel that will hold up is to buy a large, expensive big-game reel with a first-class reputation.

12

Large-, mid-, and standard-arbor reels

ONE ADDITIONAL DECISION TO MAKE WHEN CHOOSING A fly reel is the relative size of its arbor. Standard-arbor fly reels, the most traditional, wind the line on a narrow central arbor. Reeling in fifty feet of fly line when you are done for the day takes about one hundred cranks of the reel handle. And imagine how hard you'd have to reel to get control of a bonefish that suddenly decided to run toward the boat at full speed. Fly line also has a "memory" when coiled on a spool, so the narrower the arc a line is wound on, the tighter the coils. Fly reel designers got around both of these problems by making the arbor in the center of the reel wider, which not only makes the coils less severe, it also doubles the amount of line wound with each revolution of the spool. Not surprisingly, these are called "large-arbor fly reels."

All three of these reels have the same line and backing capacity. The large-arbor reel on the left is bigger but will retrieve line twice as fast as the standard-arbor reel on the right. The mid-arbor reel in the middle is a compromise between size and retrieve ratio.

Why would anyone wish for a fly reel that kinks up the line and takes in so little line with each revolution? Large-arbor reels are wider overall than standard-arbor reels, and on a light trout rod a large-arbor reel looks overpowering. Thus, for small-stream fishing with light fly rods, where casts are less than twenty feet all day long, a large-arbor reel just isn't needed. For those in-between situations (or for people that just can't make up their minds) mid-arbor reels are also made in some styles.

Spools aren't interchangeable between standard-, mid-, and large-arbor reels, but don't lose any sleep over which one you pick. I've fished for small-stream trout with large-arbor reels and for years I fished for bonefish with standard-arbor reels and never felt handicapped in either circumstance.

13

Picking the right waders

WHEN PICKING A PAIR OF WADERS, REGARDLESS OF WHAT other decisions you make, the most important point is the correct fit. Waders should be loose enough to let you do deep-knee bends without constricting your movement so you'll be able to step over logs or climb a steep bank once you get to the river, but they also should not be excessively loose, as baggy waders present more resistance to the current and

The boot-foot waders on the right come with boots already attached and are ready to use. The stocking-foot waders on the left will need a pair of separate wading shoes.

will also wear more quickly because the fabric chafes and eventually wears through. Buy waders at a store where you can try them on, or carefully study the size chart on a Web site and buy from a retailer that offers easy return privileges if they don't fit.

Get breathable waders. Clammy waders can ruin your day, and although those thick neoprene waders may look warm, your body condensation stays inside them all day long. (Besides, you can wear layers of fleece inside breathable waders and stay just as warm.) And you only have to wear neoprene waders once on a 90-degree afternoon under the blazing Montana summer sun to realize you made a big mistake.

Waders come in two basic styles: boot foot and stocking foot. With boot foots, the boot is an integral part of the wader and you just slip them over your socks. Some have laces for extra security and some are just plain rubber boots. They are the easiest waders to put on if you aren't very nimble. Stocking foot waders, which incorporate a breathable upper with neoprene booties, require a separate wading boot. They give you a lot more flexibility, so if your foot size does not correspond to what is common for your height and weight, your chances of getting a better fit are greatly increased. You can also pick a lightweight wading boot for travel or a heavier boot for more support on long walks or rocky streams.

14

What to wear under waders

EVEN IF YOU'RE A NATURAL-FIBER NUT, I URGE YOU TO put aside your cotton pants when wearing waders. Cotton absorbs sweat and condensation, and when you're exposed to the open air, cotton keeps you cool, but once trapped inside waders, cotton gets ugly. Synthetic fibers like polypropylene and nylon absorb little water or wick it away from your body, and when you take your waders off they dissipate moisture quickly.

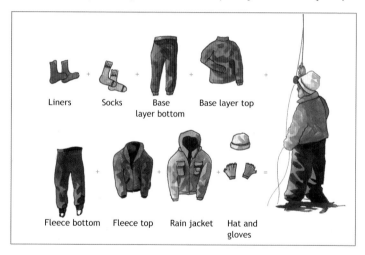

Liners   Socks   Base layer bottom   Base layer top

Fleece bottom   Fleece top   Rain jacket   Hat and gloves

Start with a pair of light wool or synthetic liner socks, adding a pair of heavier wool socks for cold water. Be careful that your socks are long enough to trap your lower pant leg, because bare skin anywhere against waders is a sure ticket to nasty skin abrasion. For warm weather, a pair of light synthetic pants of whatever style you like is perfect. For colder weather, layer a pair of thin synthetic base-layer bottoms followed by a pair of heavy fleece pants.

On top, for warm weather you can get away with anything you want—even a cotton shirt if you insist. For cold weather, layer like you do on the bottom—a thin synthetic base layer, a layer of fleece or merino wool over that, and for really cold weather follow with a thin jacket or vest. I find that knit fabrics under waders for both top and bottom are superior to woven fabrics because they stretch more and let you move easier, even when bundled up against the cold.

With proper layering, you can fish all winter in comfort.

Be careful not to overdo the top layer, as the wader top breaks the wind. It's surprising how light you can go under waders. A rain jacket is essential on cold days even if the sun shines all day, because the waterproof fabric of a rain jacket cuts the wind on the parts of your body not covered by the waders.

15

What color clothing should you wear?

RED SHIRTS ADD A GREAT SPLASH OF COLOR AND contrast to outdoor photos, but you couldn't pick a worse color for fishing. Most fish we chase with a fly rod are spooked when they see us, and blending in with the background gives you an advantage when sneaking up on the fish. For wooded streams, brown, tan, or green make you less visible, and it couldn't hurt to wear that camo shirt you typically save for opening day of dove season. In salt water, where you are silhouetted against the sky or clouds, light blue and white are the best colors. Plus, these hues keep you cooler than darker colors under the hot sun.

Mosquitoes and other biting insects are strongly attracted to the colors red and black. Blue is slightly less appealing to bugs. Light tan and light olive attract less attention from bugs than any other colors, and because these colors also help you blend into the background, they're good all-around choices for fly fishing. And you thought most of that clothing in fishing catalogs was tan and olive because fly fishers are just boring.

This orange hat and vest may not be the best choice of wardrobe for sneaking up on wary trout.

What fly line should you use for starting out?

YOUR FIRST FLY LINE SHOULD BE A TAPERED LINE OF THE size called for on your rod. And it should float. When you look at fly line designations, you'll see something like this: "WF5F." The first two letters represent the taper, which is less important and is covered in the section below on weight forward versus double taper lines. The middle number is the line size, and it must match the designation on your rod. The last letter, F, tells you the line floats, which is what you want.

Why is a floating line so important if you won't fish many dry flies? First, it's much easier to pick up a floating line off the water when you're casting than a sinking one, because you have to lift all of the line free of the water when making a cast, and getting a submerged line moving and above the water with a single back cast is difficult. Next, you can fish nearly every kind of fly—floating or sinking—with a floating line because you can use a weighted fly or weight on your leader to sink a fly, but you can't fish a dry fly with a sinking line. Third, floating lines land much lighter on the water, and when you're starting out, you'll need all the help you can muster to keep your fly line from landing on the water too hard.

For trout fishing, I use a sinking line less than 1 percent of the time, and could probably live without ever using one. A floating line is also the basic line for Atlantic salmon, bonefish, redfish, and bass, so I'm not just suggesting this line for the novice. Unless you fish for saltwater fish in deep water or fast currents, or fish for trout in lakes in midsummer after they go deep, you may go for years without feeling the need for a sinking line.

Even in deep water, you can fish with a floating line by adding weight to your leader and adjusting your presentation. ▶

When to use a sinking line

FOR MOST FLY FISHING, YOU DON'T NEED A SINKING LINE. However, when you need one, you *really* need one, most often when you are faced with water over six feet deep in combination with fast current or tides, and when you want your fly to swim close to the bottom for as long as possible. You *can* fish quite deep when fishing with a floating line, but at some point the amount of weight you need to add to your leader gets cumbersome, and when fishing deep with a floating line, as soon as you begin a retrieve the fly angles toward the surface, which is not always desirable.

Here is a situation when I always fish a fast-sinking line. When fishing offshore from a boat for striped bass, the fish are often suspended over the bottom at twenty to thirty feet, hovering around submerged structure, ambushing baitfish. Here you want your baitfish imitation to sink quickly and to swim close to the bottom, showing the fly to as many fish as possible before bringing the line to the surface for another cast. Here you need a Depth Charge line (a fast-sinking line combined with an intermediate running line behind it), a full-sinking class V line (the fastest-sinking standard fly line) or a fast-sinking shooting head.

Another instance where you want either a sinking line or a sink-tip line (a fast-sinking head, typically about fifteen feet long, followed by a floating running line that makes line pickup and mending easier) is when fishing streamers in fast water. Even if you want your fly to run shallow, stripping a streamer quickly with just a floating line makes the fly skim

When fishing the open ocean over deep water, it's almost essential to have a sinking line onboard.

across the surface, and in order to keep the fly under water you need a sinking line to help keep it down. I also use a fast-sinking line when fishing baitfish imitations over breaking fish in open ocean, because the sinking line keeps the fly running just under the waves if you begin stripping immediately after the fly hits the water.

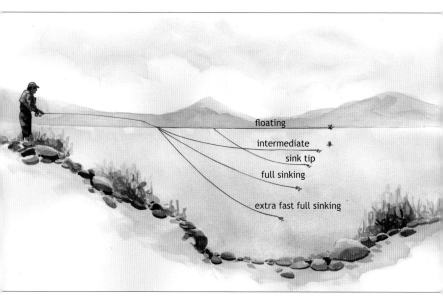

floating

intermediate

sink tip

full sinking

extra fast full sinking

If you fish for trout or bass in ponds, you always hope to find them close the surface, but if their food is deep or if the water close to the surface is too warm, fish may stay deep throughout the day. The best way to fish for trout or bass in more than twenty feet of water is to use a sinking line using the countdown method. Make a long cast and count to ten or twenty (or your lucky number if you wish) before retrieving your nymph or streamer. If you catch a fish on the first cast consider yourself lucky. Now you know how long to let your fly sink. If not, increase your count until you catch fish or hang bottom. If you hang bottom on successive casts, decrease your count by a small amount until you stop hanging up, because fish can see a fly above them but won't notice a fly that is below their level.

18

What's the difference between a weight forward and a double taper line?

THE MOST COMMON FLY LINE TAPERS ARE WEIGHT forward (WF) and double taper (DT). Both are the same for the first thirty feet of line, so if you never cast beyond thirty feet, the difference is irrelevant to you. Beyond thirty feet, weight forward lines taper for about six feet to a thinner portion called the running line, which is then level or un-tapered until the end of the line at ninety feet. Weight forward lines are best for distance casting because the thin running line offers less resistance to the wind and to the guides on the fly rod, so this line pulls extra line from your hand and propels it forward more easily. So a weight forward line seems to

A double taper line is perfect for roll casts, longer false casts, and mending line in tight spots like this.

give you the best of both worlds—the same characteristics at a short distance as a double taper, plus the ability to make long casts beyond thirty feet.

A double taper line beyond thirty feet increases in diameter very gradually to a ten-foot level section right in the middle of the line, after which it begins to slowly decrease, ending in a mirror image of the first forty-five feet of the taper. Why, with all the advantages of a weight forward line, would an angler ever want a double taper line? The bigger mass in the middle of a double taper is easier to mend once on the water so it is helpful in tricky currents. When making long (over forty-foot) false casts with a dry fly, a double taper with its gradual increase is easier to hold in the air. A double taper line roll casts beyond forty feet better than a weight forward, which loses all its power if you attempt a long roll cast because the skinny running line does not offer enough mass to keep the line moving. And, finally, when the end of a double taper line gets worn out and loses its floating qualities, the line can be reversed so it will last twice as long. Thus for someone who fishes either small streams or mostly dry flies, a double taper line lasts twice as long as a weight forward.

19

How to connect a leader to a fly line

CONNECTING A STIFF, CLEAR MONOFILAMENT LEADER TO a soft, flexible fly line requires more than your average Boy Scout knot, although when I was first learning to fly fish, one book told me to use a sheet bend knot. It was thick and clumsy and did not hold well, so once I discovered the nail knot it was a revelation. A nail knot is smooth and very strong, and when tied properly the coating will come off a fly line before the knot fails.

To make the smoothest connection of all, cut the loop off your leader (if it came with a pre-made loop, which most do these days) and nail knot the leader right to the line. However, if you want to move from a seven-and-a-half-foot leader to a twelve-footer, you have to cut off the nail knot and tie another one. This is not something you want to do a couple of times a day, and you lose a small piece of fly line very time you do. Still, if I have a fly line like a 2-weight on which I know I will always use the same leader throughout the season, I'll nail knot a leader to the line because it is the smoothest connection possible.

Nail Knot

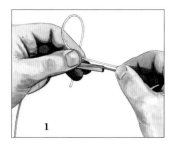

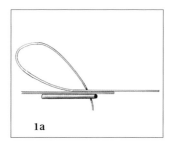

1

1a

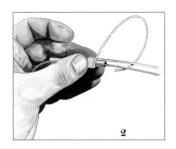

2

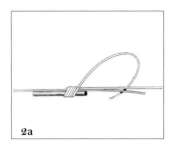

2a

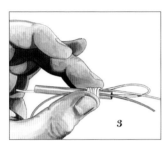

3

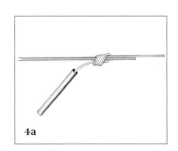

3a

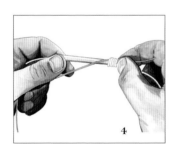

4

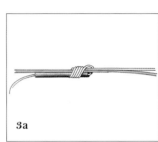

4a

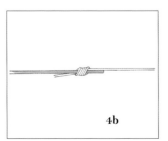

4b

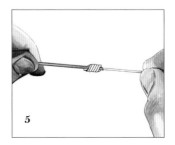

5

Many fly lines these days come with loops already attached to the end of the line. The loop might be a piece of heavy monofilament nail knotted to the line, a hollow braided loop glued to the line, or the line may be made with a self-loop at the factory where the line is pulled around and fused to itself. With a permanent loop on your line, when you want to change leaders all you do is make a simple loop-to-loop connection. No knots, nothing to trim, and pretty slim once it's cinched down. If your line did not come with a pre-made loop, just tie a six-inch piece of .023-inch nylon to the end of the fly line and tie a perfection loop on the other end.

Perfection Loop

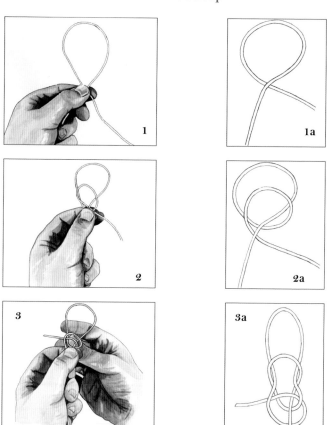

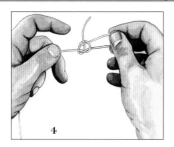

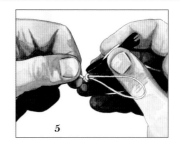

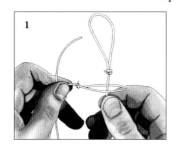

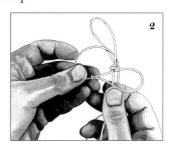

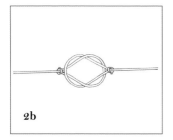

Loop to Loop

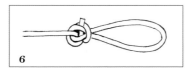

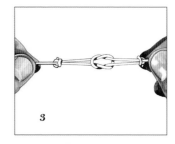

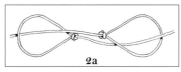

20

What is backing and how do you tie it to your reel and line?

IF YOU FISH FOR BIG TROUT OR SALTWATER FISH WITH a fly rod, sooner or later you'll run out of fly line when a fish makes a powerful run. Fly lines are ninety or one hundred feet long, and some fish will run more than a hundred yards before you can stop them. Backing is your insurance. It's thinner than fly line, so you can get lots of it on a spool. Backing comes in two flavors: braided Dacron and braided gel-spun polyester. Both are thin, supple, and strong, but gel-spun is half the diameter of Dacron in the same strength so you can pack more of it on the spool. It's also much more expensive, but if you need two hundred yards of backing on a spool but can only fit one hundred yards of Dacron on it with the fly line you want to use, you'll have to go with gel-spun.

Because most fly lines break at about twenty-five pounds, you only need twenty-pound Dacron or thirty-five-pound gel-spun (it doesn't come any smaller) backing for trout lines. Some big-game fly lines have a stronger core, so you may see fifty-pound gel-spun offered for these special lines.

When winding on backing, it's helpful to have two people—one to crank the reel and the other to hold the spool of backing on a pencil.

If you can, try to buy your fly reels already mounted with line and backing. Most fly shops have a special line-winding machine and will do it for you for free or for a modest fee. If you have to do it yourself it's time-consuming but no big deal. First tie the backing to the spool with a couple half hitches or an arbor knot. Chances are you'll never get down to the backing and will never see this knot again. Then, get a helper to put a pencil through the center of the plastic spool that holds the backing and wind it on your reel, level-winding the backing slowly back and forth over the spool arbor so it doesn't bind or cut into itself. Your helper should keep tension on the spool to make sure your winds are tight.

Arbor Knot

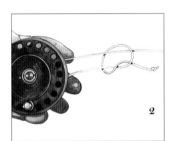

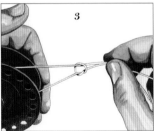

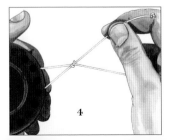
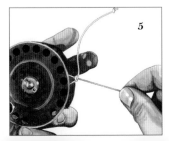

When you've wound all the backing on the spool, tie it to your fly line. The simplest way to attach backing to a fly line is with an eight-turn nail knot. It's fine for trout fishing and for smaller saltwater fish. If you're going for fish over twenty pounds, a fail-safe way to attach backing to the line is with a loop-to-loop connection. Tie a large loop in the backing with a surgeon's loop (large enough to pass the plastic fly line spool through when you make the loop-to-loop connection). Then make a self loop in the fly line by doubling the line over itself for about two inches and then securing it by tying three separate nail knots over the loop with twelve- to fifteen-pound-test monofilament. Now make a loop-to-loop connection and wind the fly line on your spool the same way you did the backing.

21

What is a tippet and what do you do with it?

THE TIPPET IS THE LAST PART OF YOUR LEADER, THE PART where you attach your fly. When you buy a new knotless leader, the tippet is an integral part of the leader, not a separate piece. Over the years, fly fishers have determined that a leader made from 25 percent heavy butt section, 50 percent quick step-down taper, and 25 percent level tippet casts best. If you run your fingers carefully down a knotless leader you can feel these transitions. The level tippet allows your fly to land softly on the water.

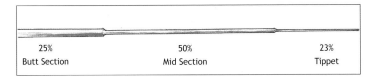

25%	50%	23%
Butt Section	Mid Section	Tippet

Sooner or later, you'll tie so many flies on the tippet that it will get too short. You'll see your fly land with a big splat, which tells you it's time for either a new leader or just a new tippet. So you can either waste a few bucks and tie on a whole new leader, or, if you're smart, you'll have spools of tippet material in your pocket so you can just tie on a new tippet with a surgeon's knot. Two to three feet is standard for a tippet—any shorter and your fly might land too hard; any longer and the leader may not straighten completely because the tippet end is too air-resistant. In general, a shorter tippet is easier to cast in the wind and a longer one is better if you're fishing in moving water with lots of conflicting currents.

You'll need a spool of tippet in the same size as your leader, and one size smaller and larger in case you decide to fish bigger or smaller flies.

Casting

22

How do you cast in the wind?

THE COMBINATION OF WIND AND FLY FISHING SCARES many people away, but with a few basic tips you can easily fish in winds up to about twenty miles per hour. Above that it does get pretty hairy. Here are some guidelines for casting on windy days:

- Keep your casts short. Spend more time getting close to fish. Fish are not as spooky on windy days so you can afford to creep right up on them.
- Cast side-armed instead of directly overhead. The wind is lighter closer to the water, and by casting at 90 degrees to the vertical you keep the fly and line farther away from your head.

- With a tailwind, put more energy into your back cast and aim it higher, and put less energy into your forward cast. With a headwind, reverse the process.
- If you have a crosswind, try to make sure the crosswind does not blow the fly across your body. Turn around and cast, or change positions.

Side-arm casting

- Shorten your leader and tippet and try to use flies that are less wind-resistant.
- On long casts with a light wind, I would rather cast into the wind that with it. I find that a wind behind me pushes my back cast below the tip of the rod and ruins my forward cast. I find it easier to let the wind help me on my back cast, and then I overpower the forward cast.

Turning your cast to the side on a windy day will give you better control of your line.

23

How do you increase the length of your casts?

MOST FISH OF ALL TYPES ARE CAUGHT AT FORTY FEET OR less, but eventually you'll need to reach out and touch a distant spot, especially if you do any fishing in salt water. The first thing to remember is that excessive false casts, which are the normal response to a long cast, are counterproductive. The more your line is in the air, the greater the chance you'll eventually screw up. Take your time and slow down. Hold some loose line in reserve, either in big coils or in a stripping basket. Increase your false casts to about thirty-five or forty feet, which is where the rod really begins to flex and pick up energy. Make no more than three false casts. On the last one,

Increasing your false casts to about forty feet and holding some line in reserve will help you make longer casts.

release the excess line and aim your rod tip slightly higher than you would on a shorter cast, to help the extra line clear the guides on the rod.

Remember that as you increase the length of line you cast, your timing will be a bit slower because it takes longer for the line to straighten behind you. Also, raise your arm up above your head and increase the length of your casting stroke. On a short cast, the rod should move mostly up and down. On a long cast, you should add length to your stroke by moving the rod back and forth in addition to up and down. Yes, you will go beyond that sacred two o'clock position you learned from your uncle, but you need the longer casting stroke to move the longer line.

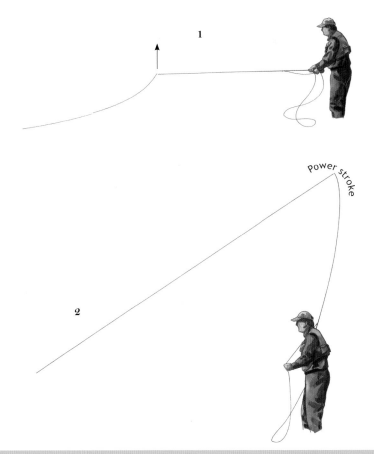

3

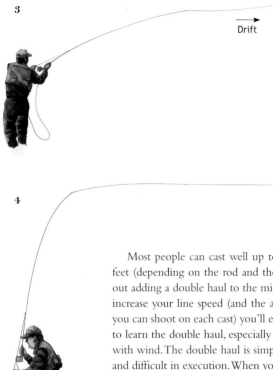

Drift

4

Most people can cast well up to fifty or sixty feet (depending on the rod and the caster) without adding a double haul to the mix. However, to increase your line speed (and the amount of line you can shoot on each cast) you'll eventually want to learn the double haul, especially if you're faced with wind. The double haul is simple in principle and difficult in execution. When you raise the rod into your back cast, you haul downward on the line with your other hand. The line hand then drifts back to meet with the casting hand as the back cast straightens, and as the rod hand moves forward on the forward cast, the line hand again hauls downward and then releases the shooting line.

There are as many styles and opinions on how much to haul and when to do it as there are casting styles. It often helps to haul on the back cast and let the line fall to the ground behind you. Then take a look at your hand position (hands

5

should be together as the back cast straightens) and make the forward cast with a haul. You'll be amazed that even with the line on the ground behind you, a decent forward cast is possible because of the increased line speed you generate with the double haul. Keep practicing it until you suddenly feel the fly line try to jump from your hands—then you've got it.

End of haul, just before releasing line

6

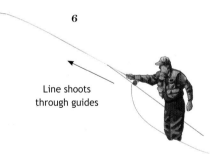

Line shoots through guides

24

How should your leader, line, and fly land on the water?

SOMEWHERE, SOMEHOW, A SUPPOSED EXPERT TOLD NOVice anglers that their fly should land on the water before the line and leader. I know this because year after year, when teaching in the Orvis fishing schools, I'd have students ask me how to make their fly land first. You can do it, but I've never figured out why you'd want to.

In order to slow down the tremendous forward speed of your line and leader so your cast does not slam on the water, you must take advantage of their air resistance. The best way to slow down the cast and present the fly with accuracy is to be sure the line, leader, and fly all straighten above the water at the same time. Two feet above the water is about right. The key to accomplishing this is to get a nice straight back cast, a quick power stroke that drives the tip of the rod forward, and then a seamless follow-through with the rod until the tip of the rod is parallel to the water.

With this nice loop straightening above the water, the line, leader, and fly will all land at about the same time, taking advantage of their air resistance.

25

Keeping your fly line slick

SMOOTH, SLICK FLY LINES CAST BETTER, SHOOT BETTER, and float better. Lines pick up dirt and algae when used, and they simply have to be cleaned. Commercial line dressings make them feel slicker at first, but these concoctions end up attracting more junk to the line's surface and defeat the purpose. Some people clean their lines after every fishing trip, while others do it once a season. The ideal frequency depends on how much algae is in the water you fish and how much you drag your line along the ground. But cleaning a line is so simple that most of us should do it more often.

Simply take a soft cloth or paper towel and wet it with warm water to which you've added a small amount of dish soap. Now strip the line off your reel in nice loose coils in a room free of cats, dogs, and small children, or outside on the lawn. Once all the line is off your reel, run it through the cloth, applying enough pressure to make the fly line squeak a little. Then work back the other way with a clean, dry cloth. You may find that once you strip off half your line it already looks slick and pristine (unless you cast the whole fly line when you fish), so you may be able to stop after about forty feet.

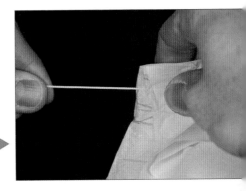

Dirt collects on the surface of the fly line and keeps it from floating and shooting well. All you have to do is wash the line in warm soapy water and run it through a paper towel to remove it.

26

How to keep from hanging up in trees and brush—and what to do about it

OKAY, LET'S FIRST ESTABLISH A FACT OF LIFE. EVERYONE gets hung up in trees or streamside brush. *Everyone*. Fly fishers who tell you different are either lying or never fish in those tricky places where the best fish lurk. All you want to do is minimize your hangups.

Keeping a few points in the back of your mind will help. For instance, the best place to position yourself in brushy streams if you are right-handed is from the middle of the river to the left bank (looking upstream) if you have the option, because most right-handers cast a little off to the right. Always look behind before you cast and make a few practice false casts. This is not just a rookie move—everybody does it. Don't forget that the longer your cast, the harder it is to control, especially on windy days, so if you keep getting hung in the trees shorten up a bit.

If (sorry, *when*) you get hung up in a tree, the worst thing you can do is to yank on your line with the rod. Yanking on a fly caught in a tree often puts a severe strain on a fly rod—one it was not designed for. Either carefully lay your rod on the bank and then pull on the line and leader with your hands, or point the tip of the rod directly at the fly and walk backward.

Everybody gets hung up in trees. This, however, is not the best way to retrieve a stuck fly. It's much better to back up, keeping the rod tip pointed directly toward the fly.

27

What rod action
do you need?

I HESITATE TO OPEN THE MESSY BOX OF JARGON THAT FLY
fishers use to describe rod actions, because few people understand what a
fly rod really does. But in the convoluted world of choices in fly rods today,
we all need guidelines besides just length and line size. You'll hear the words
fast, medium, and slow to describe rod action. To one person, fast means a
rod that bends more close to the tip than it does down into the middle of

In a small mountain stream like this, a full-flex action will load the rod better
on short casts.

the rod. To other anglers, a fast rod is one that's stiffer than others of the same configuration. Or you'll hear rods described as "still" or "soft." Orvis uses a standard that, I believe, is less confusing because it describes exactly how a rod bends under a given load, and can be measured and duplicated from one rod to the next. This system uses the terms tip-flex, mid-flex, and full-flex. A tip-flex rod bends mostly at the tip and a lot less in the middle, mid-flex bends down into the middle of the rod, and in a full-flex action, the rod bends right down into the handle.

Obviously there are degrees of each action, but putting rods in those broad terms is enough. So what do these terms tell you about what the rod will do for you? A tip-flex rod develops higher line speed and tighter casting loops, which means it is a rocket ship that will shoot a lot of line. It also has more reserve power for long casts, and most anglers feel this action has better accuracy on long casts. A full-flex rod is great for short casts and light tippets; because the rod bends so much it acts as a superb shock absorber. It's also more fun with small fish because the rod bends so easily. A mid-flex rod, naturally, is somewhere in between and is a great compromise between close-in accuracy and power for distance.

You might find you like one action type for all your rods. That's fine; one of the actions just might fit your personality and casting style. For instance, if you are a type-A person you might always want a tip-flex rod, and if it takes a life-threatening situation to get your pulse going, you might want a laid-back full-flex rod all the time. I prefer a tip-flex for saltwater fishing where I know I'll have a lot of wind and will be forced to make frequent long casts. For small-stream trout fishing I like a real full-flex action. For basic trout fishing I like a mid-flex. Fortunately, reliable fly shops will let you "try before you buy" so if you're not sure, you can experiment with different actions before you decide on the right one for you.

28

When you need a roll cast

WHENEVER POSSIBLE YOU SHOULD USE THE STANDARD overhead cast. It's more accurate, you can cast farther when you need to, and it lands on the water more softly. However, you will encounter times, especially on small streams or on bigger rivers where you can't wade out very far, when streamside brush makes a back cast impossible.

Getting ready for a roll cast in a tight spot

Also, because the roll cast does not require an existing bend in your rod in order to propel the line forward, as an overhead cast does, it's perfect for those times when for some reason you've ended up with a pile of line

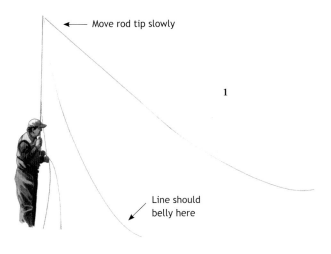

Move rod tip slowly

1

Line should belly here

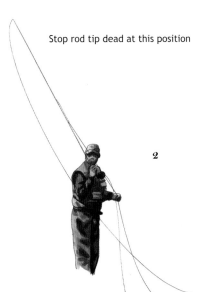

Stop rod tip dead at this position

2

at your feet. You can start with a quick roll cast to get the line out on the water in front of you. Then you'll be able to develop a bend in the rod for an overhead cast because the straight line, without slack, will begin to bend the rod immediately and will build up enough energy to flex the rod and drive the line behind you for a back cast.

The roll cast is almost intuitive and takes about five minutes to learn. Just move the rod tip back slowly until you get a semicircle of line behind the rod and slightly off to the side. A quick point with the tip of the rod will drive the line out in front of you with no back cast.

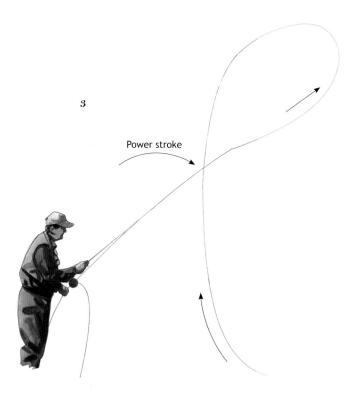

3

Power stroke

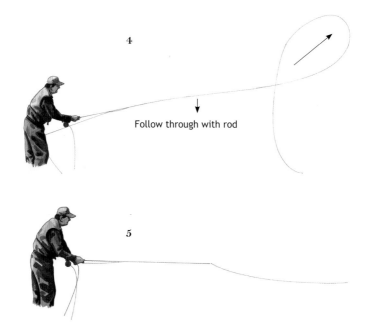

4

Follow through with rod

5

29

Why does your fly keep hitting your line?

FLY CASTERS OFTEN GET FRUSTRATED WHEN THE FLY catches the rod, fly, or leader on its path, and this happens most often on the forward cast. The first thing to check is the wind—make sure you don't have a crosswind blowing the fly into your rod. With no wind to blame, the most common reason for this problem is a closed or "tailing" casting loop.

A nice loop like this one won't catch on itself.

To understand what happens on a bad loop like this, you have to first see what happens on a good loop. Examining your own casting loop is tough. You're not at a good angle to see what's happening. My advice is to watch a good caster in action, either live or on a video. You see that a good casting loop on the forward cast looks like the letter J turned on its side, or a candy cane. As the forward cast unrolls, the bottom of the loop gets longer and the top gets shorter. In a good cast, the top loop always stays above the bottom loop. A tailing loop happens when the top of the loop drops below the bottom, and the fly catches on the line.

Tailing loop fly hits radar line

Tailing loops can be tough to correct, and the only therapy is practice. Some casters respond better to knowing what their hand and arm are doing wrong, and others find it easier to correct problems just by thinking about the rod and line. A tailing loop is usually caused by the caster using too much wrist on the forward cast, too soon. The weaker wrist muscles are better at giving the forward cast that final crisp snap, so when you make a forward cast, try to initiate the cast with your forearm and follow up with a wrist snap. If you find it easier to relate to what the rod and line are doing, remember that the tip of the rod has to get out of the way of the line quickly, and the best way to do this is to concentrate on pointing the rod straight out in front of you, at waist level, as quickly as possible.

A good tight loop

30

Why does your line pile up on the water?

THE FLIP ANSWER TO THIS QUESTION IS, "YOU ARE DOING something wrong on your cast," but, truly, almost anything you do wrong will give you puddles of line instead of a nice straight cast. However, two errors are the most likely suspects. First, examine a bad cast and determine if the line is piling right in front of the rod tip, or if it's slamming on the water some distance out from your position.

Line piling right in front of you is almost always caused by a poor back cast and then not putting enough quick power into the forward cast. When you practice casting, turn around and watch your back cast *every time*. Not putting enough power into the back cast, or dropping the rod tip too far behind you, dumps the line below the tip of the rod so that it can never form a good casting loop on the forward cast. Once you are able to drive

Great casters make full use of the rod's bend to develop casting energy.

the line up and behind you so that the line at the end of the back cast is straight and parallel to the water, it's a simple matter to point the tip of the rod quickly in front of you. It's hard to make a bad forward cast with a great back cast.

Line slamming into the water, surprisingly, does not come from too much power on the forward cast. It comes from aiming the tip of the rod *at* the water rather than straight out over the water. If the tip of your rod never drops below a horizontal angle on the forward cast, you can put as much power as you want to in the cast—your line will never slam on the water.

31

Casting from a boat

IN ONE RESPECT, CASTING FROM A BOAT IS EASIER, especially if the boat is stable enough for you to stand in, because you have more elevation above the water, so it's easier to pick up line and it's easier to keep your back cast high. However, boats present their own challenges, and if you're prepared to deal with them your time on the water will be easier.

First, most boats are full of cleats and seats and other gear that can grab your fly line when you make a cast. Try to remove as many obstructions as possible around your feet, or cover them with a wet towel or a piece of mesh if they can't be moved. Whereas most of us are pretty casual about where we strip our line when wading, when casting from a boat it helps if you pay more attention to where each length of line is placed when you're stripping it in. Some anglers like to use a stripping basket in a boat, which is a device used to catch all your excess line after stripping it in. A plastic trash

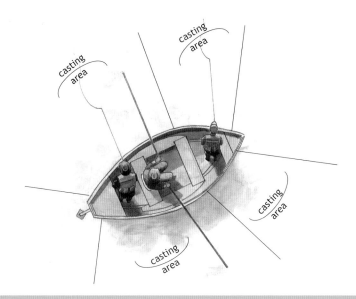

bucket can be used as a stripping basket in a pinch—just fill it with a little water to keep it weighted down and to keep your fly line slick.

You must also pay attention to the living obstructions in a boat. For instance, in a drift boat, where there is typically an angler in the bow and one in the stern with the guide sitting between the two, the territory over the length of the boat is a forbidden land—in other words, never cast straight in front of or straight behind a boat unless you want a very unhappy guide. And with two anglers casting at the same time, even if they are casting to different sides of the boat, it's very easy to tangle the back cast of one angler with the forward cast of the other. It's always the responsibility of the caster in the stern to watch out for trouble because the angler in the bow can't see what is going on behind him.

Ordinarily, the right-hander in the stern of this boat would be casting in the other direction so he could watch the other angler's back cast and not cast over the head of the guide in the middle. But all three of these guys are guides so they'll probably be OK.

Techniques

32

Which direction should you move when fishing a stream?

BEFORE YOU DECIDE WHICH DIRECTION TO FISH, YOU should have a basic strategy in mind. Will you be fishing primarily with a dry fly, nymph, wet fly, or streamer? Dry flies are best fished at an upstream angle to prevent drag, and because dry-fly fishing is usually practiced in shallow water where fish can see the surface, working against the current keeps you behind the fish, in the blind spot in their rear quarters. Swing a wet fly or a streamer on a downstream angle, and by working slowly downstream, you can cover all the likely water by swinging the fly across the current, taking a few steps downstream, and repeating the process.

This angler is swinging a wet fly downstream, making a few steps between each cast so he covers all the water.

You can fish nymphs at almost any angle you can think of, depending on water conditions and the rig you're using. The most popular way to fish nymphs is across-stream, casting on a slight upstream angle, so when fishing them you can move either upstream or downstream. If the water is shallow it's a good idea to work upstream, as you would with a dry fly, so you can sneak up on the fish. If the water is swift and it's too much work to constantly fight the current, you may prefer to move slowly downstream.

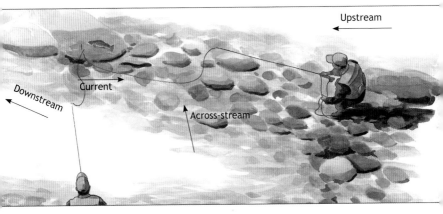

33

Do you need a net or can you use your hands?

NETS CLUTCH AT BRANCHES AS YOU WALK THROUGH THE woods and are just another piece of gear hanging from your fishing vest. Do you really need one? If all the fish you catch are smaller than twelve inches, it's probably just as easy to land the fish by hand, cradling each fish gently in the water while holding the leader and freeing the fly with a pair of forceps. However, this gets tougher as the fish get bigger and friskier, as once a fish gets close to you it takes about twice as long to maneuver it to hand as it does just to scoop it up in a net. You'll also lose more flies and more fish because of last-minute headshakes that wouldn't have occurred if the fish was already safely in a net.

Small trout can be easily handled without a net.

34

How to land a fish without losing it

MOST FISH ARE LOST AT THE STRIKE OR DURING THE FINAL moments of landing. The rest of the stuff in between might be exciting, but it's not where many fish are lost. To be sure of landing a fish, the best approach is to have a buddy with a net, preferably the long-handled variety so your assistant doesn't have to get so close to the fish or swipe the water for the fish. In a current, get your buddy downstream of your position, and once the fish gets in close, move your rod tip off to the side and downstream while the net handler holds the net under water. As soon as the fish passes above the net, a quick upward sweep captures it with a minimum of fuss. Swiping at a fish with a net is a quick path to a broken leader.

The best way to land a big fish in fast water is to have someone hold the net underwater and lead the fish over the top of the net.

Without a friend with a net, assuming you have one yourself, try to lead the fish upstream of your position with the tip of the rod, reach out and place the net under water, and then let the fish drift back in the current and lift the net under the fish. If you find yourself without a net and connected to a very large fish (or a fish that won't fit into the puny net you're carrying), the best approach is to beach the fish. Scan the shore for a shallow beach where you can lead the fish until it gets into water so shallow that is has to turn on its side. Once it does, you can back up and slide it easily into shallower water where it can't move at all.

During a close-quarters battle, whether from a boat in deep water or in a current while wading, remember that a fish can only swim in the direction its head is pointing. It is not easy merely to crank in a big fish, and it requires a lot less force to just turn the fish's head. Keeping the rod high over your head and pointed directly at the fish gives the fish only one option—to swim away from you and down, and any time the fish gains distance from you the fight will be longer. Keeping your rod to one side or another leads the fish back and forth, but it has to swim on an angle toward you if you keep its head pointed in your direction.

35

How long should your leader be?

YOUR HEIGHT AND THE LENGTH OF YOUR ROD HAVE NO bearing on the proper leader length. It's determined entirely by fishing conditions. When using sinking lines, you should keep the fly relatively close to the fly line, because the sinking line keeps the fly swimming deep enough and a long leader may allow the fly to rise to the surface. So here, a leader of between four and six feet is about right. Don't worry about spooking the fish with your fly so close to the line—if the fish were really spooky you would not be using a clumsy sinking line anyway.

In small streams, where line speed is slower and drifts are very short, you seldom need a leader longer than seven and a half feet unless the pools are flat and calm and fish are spooky. The short leader straightens more easily on short casts. Freshwater bass are also not shy of the fly line or leader, and you can get way with the easier-casting seven-and-a-half-footer.

Basic trout fishing with dry flies and nymphs in most rivers is done with a nine-foot leader. This length keeps the fly line far enough

On flat, clear water like this, a twelve-foot leader will help ▶ prevent spooking wary trout.

away from spooky trout, yet is easy to straighten, even in a stiff breeze. Most saltwater fly fishing is also done with nine-foot leaders, except for bonefish, redfish, or striped bass feeding in clear, shallow water, where a twelve-foot leader may give you a slight edge in stealth. Twelve-foot leaders or longer are best when fishing for trout in lakes with a floating line, because in the smooth water of a lake's surface a trout can spot a fly line landing from a long way off. And in still pools on rivers, where conditions approach those of a lake, a twelve-foot leader may be a wise move.

Under conditions of extreme low water and very spooky fish, trout anglers may also go as long as an eighteen-foot leader by adding a few feet to the butt section and to the tippet of a leader. These ultra-long leaders are helpful in keeping the fly line well away from the fish, and in making conflicting currents less of a problem with drag because a leader is suppler than a fly line. However, an eighteen-footer requires nearly perfect casts to avoid frustration, and a mere whisper of a wind can blow one well off course, so don't try one until you've developed your casting skills.

36

How to avoid upsetting other people on the water

I STILL CRINGE WHEN I THINK OF THE TIMES AS A TEENAGER when I waded right up the middle of a river where other people were fishing. I wasn't arrogant or confrontational, I just didn't know any better; but I must have raised the blood pressure of more than one fly fisher and I'm surprised I never got into an altercation. Somebody should have set me straight.

Your first rule of consideration starts before you even approach the water. If someone is already at a parking spot and getting suited up to fish, the right thing to do is to ask which direction he or she intends to go. If the other angler heads upstream, you have an obligation to go downstream. Never race to put on your gear to try to beat someone to the best water if he or she was there before you. It's just poor manners.

If you have to walk past other anglers to get to an un-crowded spot, stay as far away from the bank as you can. Walking close to the bank or in the

When a number of anglers are in a large pool, try to keep as much distance from others as possible.

shallows can spook fish and you'll spoil the fishing for people who got there before you. And if you have to cross a river, do so in shallow riffles where no one is fishing, rather than slogging through the deeper water, pushing out waves that may frighten every fish in a pool.

Always try to find a pool or a stretch of water with no one in it. Most fly fishers enjoy their solitude, whether wading a river, paddling a kayak, or walking a lonely beach. Only enter a piece of water close to another angler if he or she invites you in—otherwise give everyone a wide berth. Fly fishers move around a lot, and just because a piece of water is empty does not mean it offers poor fishing. Besides, you may find a secret hot spot that everyone else has passed up.

37

In lakes, what do you do once the fly hits the water?

ALTHOUGH IT'S SMARTER FOR A FLY FISHER TO LEARN ON a pond before advancing to the complexities of flowing water, it's usually not what happens. Most fly fishers begin as stream trout anglers, and when faced with a huge expanse of water without current to move the fly or tighten the line, they're lost.

First, slack line is never desirable on a pond, as it sometimes is in moving water. So once the fly lands, take up any slack by stripping in some line. The best way to fish a dry fly on a pond, especially if fish are rising, is to let the fly sit there without any motion. This can get boring without any fish in the vicinity, so the key to fishing a dry in still water is to move the boat close to the fish and then try to anticipate their path and get your fly in front of them. Otherwise it's about as interesting as picking knots out of your leader. Largemouth and smallmouth bass will also attack a fly that has remained motionless for minutes, especially if the fly has rubber legs that keep wiggling long after the fly has landed.

But most flies fished on still water are manipulated by the angler. After casting, strip in line, keeping the rod tip low and pointed straight at the fly to make the fly swim through the water, until it gets about twenty feet away. Then pick up and make another cast. If no fish or obvious cover are in sight, cast at different angle until you've covered all the water within the reach of your casting skills. Experiment with retrieve speeds as well. Small nymphs imitate tiny insects or

In lakes, after you complete a cast the rod tip should stay close to the water's surface.

crustaceans that can't swim very fast, so strips should be short and slow; streamers imitate baitfish that swim at a faster clip, so longer, faster movements might be in order. But there are always those days when a streamer works better with a slow, steady strip and a nymph catches more fish when streaking through the water. It always pays to experiment.

38

Is it worth fishing an area with canoe or boat traffic?

IN A WORD, NO, IF YOU CAN HELP IT. MOST GAMEFISH, especially trout and shallow-water saltwater species like bonefish and striped bass, are wary animals, and when faced with a lot of boat traffic they either move elsewhere or stay hidden and refuse to feed. This doesn't mean you have to give up. Look for coves out of the main boat channel in lakes and saltwater shorelines, or look for side channels too shallow for boat traffic in rivers. Sometimes, fish bigger than you'd expect will live in these less-than-optimum spots in order to avoid disturbance. The other alternative is to fish at night or in early morning, when low boat traffic makes fish less nervous and more likely to feed.

In a river with lots of boat traffic, you might have better luck in a small side channel that the boats have not disturbed.

39

Releasing fish properly

THE BEST WAY TO RELEASE ANY KIND OF FISH IS WITH A minimum of handling out of the water and gentle cradling in clean water until the fish regains enough strength to swim off on its own. One of the worst things you can do is to play a fish to exhaustion. Always use a tippet strong enough to play a fish quickly, bringing it to hand while it is still "green," not half-dead and swimming on its side. A net and a pair of forceps help keep a fish immobile in the water while you remove the hook, and of course barbless hooks are much quicker to remove. If you do handle the fish, keep your fingers away from its delicate gills and wet your hands before handling it, which helps maintain the protective mucus layer on a fish's skin.

The best way to release a fish is to hold it in clear water until it is able to swim away strongly under its own power.

One of the biggest impediments to fish survival is the famous "hero shot," where a fish is held out of the water for many minutes while the happy angler gets ready and the cameraman gets into position. First, the person with the camera should get ready while you're still fighting the fish, and you should both plan the shot before the fish is landed, taking into account background and sun angle so you don't have to reposition while the fish is out of the water. Because fish should be removed from the water for only a few seconds or not at all to ensure survival, if you really want a nice shot, try bending down and cradling the fish in the water, close to the surface. Not only are photographs like this safer for the fish, they're more interesting than a fish held out at arm's length like a bowling trophy.

Be prepared to revive a fish for as long as you played it. Many tired fish, when just thrown back in the water, go belly-up and can't maintain their equilibrium. Apparently their gills do not work properly when they are upside-down, so they can drown if not kept upright. Find an area of clean water with slight waves or moderate current that completely covers the fish. Cradle its head and belly with your hands and gently move it back and forth to get water moving across its gills. When a fish is ready to move off on its own, it will let you know by breaking free of your gentle embrace.

40

What is drag and how do you stop it?

THE EASIEST WAY TO DESCRIBE DRAG IS TO DEMONSTRATE when it is absent. Throw a twig into moving water and watch how it floats—it moves at the mercy of each little micro-current on the surface, never cutting across currents of different speed. This is how an insect drifts. Few insects have the power to swim contrary to any amount of current, and the movements they do make are tiny hops and pirouettes, not enough to throw off a wake. A fly that creates a wake telegraphs a message to a feeding fish that the object in question is not food because it does not behave like the rest of the insects.

When attached to a leader, a fly can streak across currents when the leader or line is in a different current than the fly. This will happen, eventually, on every cast you make, and avoiding drag is merely ameliorating what must happen when something is attached to a floating object. Drag can be very overt, when you can see the wake from thirty feet away, or it can be minuscule, arising from tiny current threads and invisible to an observer just a few feet from the fly. But trout can always see it.

The best way to avoid drag is to fish in uniform currents and cast straight upstream. If the line and leader float at exactly the same speed as the fly, drag won't develop until the fly is almost even with your rod tip. But fishing straight upstream is often not practical or even desirable, because on a long drift it puts your fly line right on top of the fish. So most times when fishing with a dry fly or nymph we cast at an angle that is somewhere between straight upstream and directly across the current. At this angle you'll often get a decent drag-free float for four or five feet. However, you'll often be faced with trout feeding in slow water along the far bank and fast water between you and the fish, so without some tricky moves you might get only an inch of drag-free float. Here are some of the tricks to use, either alone or in combination:

- Change positions. Often just moving a few feet will give you a longer drag-free float.
- Instead of fishing quartering upstream, fish quartering downstream. If you can, also make a quick mend upstream just before your line hits the water. This is called a reach cast, and that upstream arc in your line has to invert before the fly drags.
- Add an extra-long tippet to your leader. The tippet will land in loose coils, which will have to straighten before your fly begins to drag.
- Make a sloppy cast. By this I don't mean one that slams on the water, but an underpowered cast of controlled sloppiness that throws big piles of slack line on the water. You'll have to cast more line than you think you need because some of your line will be taken up in the loose piles on the water.

Slow current
or
Dead water

Fast current

Fly drags

41

What is the best way to wade a fast river?

PEOPLE DROWN EVERY YEAR WHILE WADING IN RIVERS. Most of these accidents are preventable. The first rule is to always wear a wader belt. Waders with air trapped inside them are quite buoyant (no, you won't float upside down and drown; Lee Wulff proved that eighty years ago by jumping off a bridge while wearing waders) and by keeping the belt tightly cinched around your waist, you'll hold a lot of air inside. Besides, in a moderate spill you'll only get wet from the waist up.

The best way to fish a treacherous river like this is to shuffle your feet slowly, keep your profile sideways to the current, and never wade downstream when you don't know what's below you.

In addition, keep these tips in mind to avoid an accident:

- When crossing fast water, always angle upstream. You will be sure you can retrace your steps to safety, whereas if you wade downstream in fast current and find yourself pushed into a deep hole, you may not be able to retreat.

- The best places to cross are in riffles and the tails of pools, where the water is shallowest.

- Keep your profile sideways to the current to present less resistance to the water.

- Use a wading staff, which adds amazing security and balance to your wading. If you don't have one and need to cross some raging currents, find a hefty stick to use as a temporary staff. It's like growing a third leg.

- Shuffle your feet along the bottom, making sure your forward foot has a secure spot before moving your other foot forward.

- Look for patches of sand and gravel, which typically show up as lighter spots on the bottom. They are much easier to negotiate than rounded boulders. (It goes without saying that you should wear polarized glasses so you can see below the surface better.)

42

What to do if you hook yourself or someone else

SOONER OR LATER YOU WILL HOOK YOURSELF OR someone else. Hopefully you always wear a hat and some kind of eyeglasses so that you will not be removing a hook from a dangerous place. Barbless hooks remove as easily from human skin as they do from fish jaws, so using them is an important component of safety. But sooner or later you'll forget to de-barb a hook, or someone fishing with a barbed fly will hook you, and it's important to know how to proceed.

First, if the hook is in an eye or anywhere near it, I probably don't have to tell you get to the emergency room quickly. There is nothing you can do in this circumstance except get qualified medical care.

If the fly is lodged in an arm, cheek, or leg, the procedure for removing even a barbed hook is surprisingly easy and painless. Get a loop of strong monofilament line, about ten inches long. Place the monofilament around the bend of the hook so the open end of a loop is facing away from the eye of the fly. Wrap the open ends of the loop around your index finger. Now, while pushing straight down on the eye of the fly, give a firm, quick jerk on the monofilament. The fly will pop right out, with a minimum amount of tissue damage. Wash the wound with some type of antiseptic and make sure your tetanus shots are current.

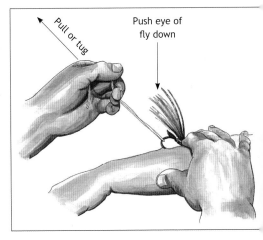

Pull or tug

Push eye of fly down

43

Where should you hold your rod tip after casting?

A GOOD CAST REQUIRES A NICE FOLLOW-THROUGH OF the rod tip, with it ending up comfortably at waist level, parallel to the water. This is especially important when practicing, as there seems to be a natural tendency to then point the tip back up to about the ten o'clock position. I think this comes from those of us who learned to fish with a spinning rod before we learned fly casting. But this causes problems most times, as when the tip is up there swinging in the breeze it moves the line backward from where you just carefully placed it with your cast, and it leaves a big loop of line in front of you to be shoved around by the wind.

In all cases when fishing in still water, saltwater or fresh, your rod tip should move down to the surface of the water after casting. Here you have more control over your fly line, and in fact some bonefish guides recommend that you put the tip just under the surface of the water and keep it there when retrieving your fly. When fishing moving water, if you are swinging a fly downstream or making a long cast in uniform current, then again your rod tip should be held low. However, if you're fishing in places with lots of swirling currents, or if the place your fly lands is in a different current lane than where you're standing, it makes sense to hold the rod higher—high enough to keep the different current between you and your fly isolated from the fly line.

A low rod tip like this keeps your line under control, especially when fishing a streamer.

44

Why do you keep breaking off fish?

THE MOST OBVIOUS CULPRIT WHEN BREAKING OFF FISH is that the fish was just too big for the tippet you were using. That might be the case, especially when you strike in a proper manner (raising the tip of the rod or making a long quick strip just until you feel tension), especially if the fish is moving away from you when it strikes. But most fish break off due to operator error.

Many fish break the tippet because of poor knots. When you break off a fish, carefully examine the part that returns to you: a curlicue in the end of

To hook and hold large fish like this brown trout, the most important thing you can do is tie knots properly.

the tippet means the knot used to tie on the fly was not tightened properly, and a missing tippet with a pigtail in the end of the leader means your tippet-to-leader knot was defective. If your tippet comes back with a clean break in the middle of it, you may have gotten a "wind knot" in the middle of it, an overhand knot that gets tied in your leader, usually due not to the wind but to poor casting technique. We call them wind knots to make ourselves feel better. Inspect your tippet often for these little overhand knots and replace your tippet if you see them, because plain overhand knots cut the strength of your tippet in half.

Sometimes the tippet material you've chosen is too light for the fly and rod you're using. Tying a 6X tippet to a size 6 streamer gives you problems because the fine tippet just won't knot well against the much bigger diameter wire used on a size 6 streamer hook. And an 8-weight rod has so much mass and backbone compared to a 4-weight trout rod that you might break a 6X tippet when striking fish no matter how careful you are.

V

Flies

Should you use barbless hooks? Why do they come barbed?

BARBLESS HOOKS ARE TERRIFIC FOR MANY REASONS. IF you hook yourself or another angler they slip out of your shirt or your anatomy without further damage. When you hook a fish with a barbless hook, backing it out of a fish's tough jawbone with a pair of forceps or pliers is almost effortless, which allows you to release a fish without even touching it, and will save you flies because many flies are lost at the last moment when trying to work a barbed hook free—the tippet breaks and away swims your fly. Fish caught on barbless hooks seldom work free as you expect they might, and because a barb presents some resistance to penetration, a barbless hook actually penetrates better than a barbed one.

Barbs are found on most fly hooks mainly because of tradition—not much has changed in hook design in the past fifty years, and some anglers still feel (needlessly) insecure without a barb on the hook. But don't worry; it's easy to remove the barb on any hook. With a pair of fine-nose pliers or forceps with flat jaws, crimp the barb flat. You can leave a small hump on the hook to act as a mini-barb if it makes you feel more comfortable, or you can flatten the barb all the way.

It's easy to make any fly barbless. Just crimp the barb flat with a pair of smooth-jawed forceps or small pliers.

46

How do you know what size fly to use?

WHETHER YOU'RE FISHING FOR TROUT OR TUNA, FLY SIZE is more important than color or pattern. When fish get selective about what they eat, the most obvious clue to the fraudulent nature of your fly will be that it's much bigger or much smaller than what they're eating. Shape is sometimes almost as important, but most experienced fly fishers feel that color is a distant third. Flies come in a wide range of sizes and you often have to experiment with different sizes before finding the right fly, but here are some tried-and-true guidelines.

- If you observe fish eating an insect or baitfish, try to capture a sample and place it alongside your fly. Minnows in the water and insects in the air often look far bigger than their true size.

- If you have to guess at the correct size, err on the smaller side. Fish are less suspicious of a fly that is smaller than what they are eating than one that is bigger. Common sense suggests that they'd want the bigger mouthful but empirical evidence suggests the opposite.

- If you don't see fish eating anything, look in the water. Look for baitfish and crustaceans in lakes and saltwater estuaries, or turn over a few rocks in a stream and look for aquatic nymphs. (Even if you'll be fishing dry flies, the insects will be hatching from nymphs of about the same size.) Pick a fly that is the same size as the most abundant prey you see.

- When fishing for big trout, bass, pike, or other species that ambush their food, try a small fly, something between one and two inches long, first. If that fails, try something twice as big. The same holds true when fishing for migratory species like salmon or steelhead that feed infrequently or not at all.

The Rusty Spinner is a great dry fly, but you'll need an assortment of sizes to match the natural insects you see.

47

How to keep a dry fly floating

IF YOU WANT TO DO THE BEST JOB OF KEEPING YOUR DRY fly floating high, resign yourself to carrying two different kinds of fly dressing. Initially, you'll want to treat your flies with some kind of waterproofing—the best is the liquid kind you apply the night before, because it really penetrates the fly with silicone and the coating lasts longer. But most of us never know what fly we'll be using the next day, or just can't be bothered thinking that far ahead.

At streamside, you should first apply a standard fly floatant. It comes in a paste version that you rub into a fly or a liquid potion for dipping or spraying. All work well, but you should apply these dressings to a *dry* dry fly, in other words, one that has not touched the water yet. Otherwise they don't coat the fly very well. Once a fly gets wet, or if you catch a fish and the fly is covered with fish slime, reapplying a standard floatant doesn't work well. That's the time to introduce your second type of floatant, a dry white powder made from ground silicates and other compounds. This second type actually draws water and slime out of a fly and applies a fine coating of water-repellent powder to the fly. If you've forgotten this second type of floatant, the next best thing to rejuvenate a drowned fly is to squeeze it into a cotton shirt or handkerchief—not as high-tech and not quite as effective, but it will do in a pinch.

A couple of short, crisp false casts, of course, always help to flick moisture off your fly. And if all else fails, use a fly made from closed-cell foam. They'll float all day without a speck of fly dressing.

A bottle of white desiccant powder is your best friend when fishing dry flies.

48

How to pick flies out in a shop

ALL FLIES ARE NOT CREATED EQUAL, EVEN THE SAME pattern in the same bin in a fly shop. Flies are still made by hand, one at a time, and since you'll be paying upward of two bucks for each one it's worthwhile to be picky when selecting them. The first thing to look for is symmetry. Nearly everything fish eat has bilateral symmetry and a fly that is lumpy on one side does not look natural to the fish. And a streamer fly or saltwater fly that is not symmetrical will not swim properly in the water and may even put twists in your tippet.

Next, look at the eye of the hook. It should be free of material or cement; otherwise you'll have trouble tying it on once you hit the water. Heads on flies should be neat and shiny, showing that enough head cement or epoxy has been used to seal the final wraps of fly-tying thread. On streamers, bass flies, and saltwater flies, yank on the wing and tails of the fly. If they pull out you obviously don't want that fly. Also hope that the fly shop owner does not have a "you break it, you buy it" philosophy (I've never met one that does). Hackles on dry flies should be uniform, stiff, and shiny. If the hackles on a fly are of uneven length or if they look dull, the fly will not float well.

For flies made out of deer hair or other bulky materials, or those made with dumbbell eyes like Clouser Minnows, the biggest test of a superior fly is to grab the fly by the bend of the hook and twist the fly. A perfectly tied fly will not twist around the hook shank, but one that does will fall apart easily and will also twist during casting, putting the fly off balance and almost certainly turning off the fish.

When picking out flies in a shop, look for symmetry, which indicates a well-tied fly.

49

How to sharpen a hook

FLY-TYING HOOKS ARE MADE FROM GOOD STEEL AND ARE coated to resist rust, but they still rust if put away wet, and delicate hook points can get out of alignment like the blade on a knife. Check your point often, especially when fishing around rocks. I can't tell you how many times I've missed several fish in a row, blaming the fish or my reflexes until I happened to check the point of my hook and found it was bent. The best way to check a hook point is to drag it across your thumbnail—if it sticks or scratches, the point is fine, but if the point just slides across the nail, you'll miss the next big fish that strikes.

A diamond file works best for bigger hooks and saltwater flies, while a fine diamond file, Arkansas whetstone, or fine ceramic will put a fine point on a small trout fly. Begin on the bottom of the hook point, stroking the fly against the sharpening surface, with the point angling just slightly into the stone. Next take a couple of licks against each side of the point. Test the hook on your nail and if it doesn't stick, repeat the process.

A good hook sharpener is cheap and fits easily in your pocket or tackle bag. It can save you hundreds of dollars a year in rescued flies, but I'd be willing to bet not one in five anglers carries a hook hone when fishing.

This rusty hook won't penetrate very well, but a few strokes with a hook hone against the point will get it back into shape.

How to thread a fly if you have poor eyesight

WHEN YOU HIT THE MAGIC AGE OF FORTY IT'S ALMOST preordained that the eyes of flies seem to get smaller. And even young eyes have trouble threading a 7X tippet to a size 22 in failing light. Sooner or later you'll need some optical assistance, and the keys to keeping your sanity are light and magnification. Anyone who plans to fish later than 6:00 p.m. should always carry a headlamp or similar tiny flashlight that can be secured to a pocket or hat to direct light in front of you while keeping your hands free. If you somehow find yourself in fading light without a flashlight, try holding the fly up against the light of the sky.

But magnification is the real key for older eyes, and you'll probably find that those 1.5X bifocal adjustments you have on your regular glasses just don't cut it for tying on a small fly, even in bright sunlight. For fly fishing, you really need 3X or 4X magnifiers, and although these powers are not

These three are all young guides and don't need close-up glasses to tie on the last fly of the day. You may not be as lucky.

easily found in drugstore readers, fly shops sell many different styles. One is a loupe device that clips to eyeglasses, making you look like Colonel Klink in *Hogan's Heroes,* but it gets the job done. Another clips to the brim of a hat and flips down when you need it. If you choose to wear a more conventional style of reading glasses, make sure you have them attached to a lanyard around your neck or you'll donate several to the stream bottom before you wise up.

Another tip is to make sure that the end of the tippet you are trying to thread is cut straight and clean. An end that is not cut with sharp snips is duller and wider, and a curled tippet is much harder to thread than a straight one. If repeated tries to thread a fly fail, it helps to run the point of another hook inside the eye of the fly in case there is something blocking the eye. (Many fly fishers' snips also incorporate a small needle just for this purpose.)

Finally, if you're into gadgets, there are many clever products designed to help thread a fly. Most work very well and it's just a matter of finding one that you're comfortable with. Try to test drive a couple at your local fly shop before buying.

51

Should you wear a fishing vest or an alternative?

SOONER OR LATER YOU'LL NEED A PLACE TO CARRY YOUR fly boxes, extra reel spools, fly floatants, strike indicators, flashlight, lunch, raincoat, water bottles, and all the other paraphernalia that fly fishers accumulate. The traditional way to carry all that stuff is a fishing vest, and although when filled up they are sometimes constricting, vests work well enough if you don't plan on hiking up and down canyon walls. However, more active fly fishers favor alternatives to vests. One is a waist pack, which is fine for small streams and wading shallow saltwater flats, but not much use when wading deep. A chest pack is a stripped-down version of a vest and typically has more storage in the back, which keeps out of the way gear to which you don't need frequent access. Some chest packs incorporate full backpacks, so if you're hiking a long way and don't want to wear your waders on the trail you can stow them until you reach the water. One of the best alternatives for the minimalist is a sling pack that you can swivel in front to grab a fly box, then push back out of the way while fishing.

Not only is a chest pack less bulky than a vest when wading, it's also easier to use on a boat.

VI

Trout

52

Do you have to match a hatch to catch trout?

UNLIKE HUMANS, TROUT DO NOT LIKE VARIETY IN THEIR diets. Feeding exposes them to predators, and eating something novel that may or may not provide useful calories could be a waste of energy. So they eat what is safe, which means familiar or abundant prey. Of course they do experiment or they'd never find a new source of food, but if a recognizable morsel is available they'll invariably choose it.

So when a particular species of insect is hatching in great numbers, trout may pay attention only to something that is similar in size, shape, and color, ignoring everything else. In that case you will do best trying to match the hatch. However, during the course of most days trout feed on a number of species of insects, crustaceans, and baitfish, and in that case they'll strike a wide variety of flies as long as the flies are within a range of what they've eaten recently. For example, several weeks after a killing frost has retired all the grasshoppers for the season, I've been able to tempt trout with a grasshopper imitation. From my experience I've found that trout keep the memory of a prey item as "safe" for about three weeks.

Sometimes there may be several insects hatching at the same time and trout may be picking off all of them. In that case, chances are if you fish a fly that looks at least close to one of the bugs you see on the water and your presentation is realistic, you'll do okay. So unless trout are feeding heavily and there appears to be only one insect present, you may not have to worry about matching the hatch.

There are times when your fly has to be close to the natural as this Sparkle Dun is to the natural mayfly. But many times it's not as critical, especially when a number of different insects are on the water.

53

Do you need to change the way you fish for different trout species?

THERE'S A COMMON MISCONCEPTION THAT BROWN trout are more likely to feed on the surface than other species of trout, but I have never found that to be true. All the common species of trout—brook, brown, rainbow, and cutthroat—feed on the surface enthusiastically when hatching insects are abundant or when land insects like ants or grasshoppers fall into the water. However, brown trout larger than sixteen inches are far more likely to eat bigger prey like minnows and crayfish, and are more likely to become nocturnal feeders than the other species. A very large brown trout may only feed on insect hatches once a month, lying low in tangled roots or submerged rocks, ambushing a big piece of meat only a few times each week, most likely after dark.

Rainbow trout often delight us because they are more efficient than any other species in converting food energy to body weight, and thus are more likely to feed all day long, sampling every likely tidbit that floats by. Rainbows will suspend in fast water and snack even when insect hatches are sparse, while brown trout may only respond to an insect hatch when food is truly abundant—thus the old saw that rainbow trout "like" fast water more than other species. They don't like it better; they're just able to feed efficiently in water that would exhaust other species.

Brook and cutthroat trout are often considered "dumber" that browns and rainbows because they appear to be easier to fool. Both of these species originated in ecosystems that are not as rich in food as the coastal streams that rainbows evolved in, or the rich European lakes and meadow streams where the introduced brown trout originally came from. So the flies originally used for these species were bright and gaudy. But a big cutthroat in a rich tailwater or a brook trout in a productive spring creek can be every bit as "smart" and selective as a brown trout, and will ignore gaudy flies.

The character of a river and its food supply are far more important than what species are present in determining what fishing techniques you should employ. However, over the years I have found a few maxims that seem to hold true:

- Rainbow trout will inhabit faster water than brown, brooks, or cutthroats.

- Brook trout are more sensitive than other species to high water temperatures; thus, when river temperatures get above 65 degrees Fahrenheit they will be found close to springs or in headwater streams where the water stays colder.

- Big cutthroat trout take a dry fly very slowly, and if you're used to fishing for other species you may pull the fly away from them if you don't slow down on your strike.

- Brown trout are very deliberate when taking a fly, and if you "miss" one, chances are it refused your fly at the last moment.

- Brown trout are more likely to feed heavily between dusk and dawn than other species.

- Brown trout, especially big ones, are more likely to take a streamer fly than other species.

- Rainbow trout often feed in "pods," so if you catch one chances are good that more are nearby.

Brook trout

Brown
trout

Cutthroat
trout

Rainbow
trout

54

Where to find trout around rocks

THE NATURAL PLACE TO LOOK FOR TROUT AROUND A BIG rock in the middle of a river is behind the rock, where the fish are protected from the brunt of the current. However, the force of the current also digs a trench in front of a midstream rock and along its sides, and a cushion of low-velocity water also builds up in front of a rock. Trout will lie in all of these places, so when fishing around big rocks it's important to make accurate casts behind a rock first, then a few casts to each side, and finally in front of the rock. By starting downstream behind the rock first you'll avoid spooking trout in front of the rock with your fly line.

55

Getting started in nymph fishing

IN MOST TROUT STREAMS, NYMPH FISHING IS THE MOST reliable way to catch trout. Surface feeding exposes trout to predators, so unless enough insects cover the surface to make this risk worthwhile, trout stay deeper in the water column and pluck food at their level. The best way to get started in nymph fishing is with a strike indicator, because not only will it let you see when fish take your fly, it will also give you an idea of where your fly is drifting, and whether your artificial is dragging across currents in an unnatural way.

Try to keep your initial nymph rig as simple as possible. Tie a weighted nymph or a beadhead pattern to the end of your tippet and then attach a strike indicator on the upper part of your leader. The indicator should be one and a half to two times the water depth up on your leader because the

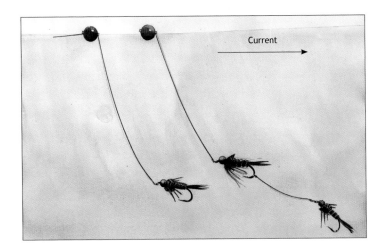

Current

fly seldom hangs straight down, and you want your fly to be suspended a few feet off the bottom. Cast at an upstream angle and watch the indicator like a heron stalking fry in the shallows. If it hesitates, wiggles, or darts upstream set the hook instantly—it's easy to miss unseen strikes to a nymph, so better safe than sorry.

Nymphs seldom drift as deep as you think, so if you don't hang up on the bottom on a dozen casts, you are probably not fishing deep enough. To get deeper, either move the strike indicator higher on your leader or add a couple split shot to the tippet about ten inches above the fly. Once you feel comfortable with a nymph rig, add a second fly by tying sixteen inches of tippet to the bend of the upper hook and adding a second fly to this piece. Two weighted flies often help you get deeper without adding shot to the tippet, and you can fish two different patterns to find out which one the trout prefer.

The Copper John is one of the most popular nymphs used, and features a wire body, brass head, peacock feathers for the thorax, and partridge feathers for the legs.

56

How to plan your first trout-fishing trip

IF YOU'VE NEVER FISHED FOR TROUT WITH A FLY ROD, your first trip should be with a guide. Guides do much more than row a boat and show you the best spots. Most fly-fishing guides are excellent teachers and will help you with every aspect of fishing, from rigging your leader to making the right presentation to landing the fish. The guide will have all the equipment you need, so you won't have to worry about having the right flies or leaders or strike indicators. A day with a guide may seem expensive at first, but consider it an investment in your education.

Fishing with a patient guide will help you learn and have a much more satisfying experience on your first trip.

When planning where to go, avoid trout streams that are described as "technical" or "spring creeks." These places usually offer challenging fishing. And I'd also stay away from waters that are famous for big trout, because many places with big trout don't have as many trout, and because these places attract lots of fishing pressure and thus the fish get smart in a hurry.

57

How do you know what insect the fish are taking?

WHENEVER YOU SEE TROUT RISING, IT'S IMPORTANT TO figure out what insects are *on* the water, not what bugs you see flying. Often, one type of insect is hatching while another variety is migrating upstream, and the ones most visible to you may not be on the water at all. This is particularly common with caddisflies, because these moth-like aquatic insects, while very important to trout, live for weeks after they hatch and migrate upstream in clouds that sometimes obscure the far bank. If you see caddisflies in the air, moving purposefully upstream in a straight line, chances are they're migrating. If you see them flying in a slow, erratic pattern, or if you see them bouncing on the water's surface, they are more likely to be hatching or returning to the water to lay eggs, and thus available to the trout.

You can tell a lot about what a trout is eating by the way it rises. This brown trout (can you spot it just to the left of the rise?) is probably taking something very small or an emerging insect in the surface film because the rise is very subtle.

Often you'll find a large insect hatching along with smaller, more abundant ones. It's natural to pay more attention to the bigger fly (and perhaps also wishful thinking because big flies are easier to see), but if the smaller flies are more abundant the trout may be eating them and ignoring the big juicy ones. It doesn't make sense to us, but when trout zero in on one insect they may ignore all others, despite how good the big ones look.

Try to watch a fish rising to see what it takes. This is not as easy as it sounds, but if you can find a fish that is rising steadily, focus in on that spot until you can figure out what the fish are taking. Some anglers carry a pair of pocket-sized binoculars just for this purpose. If you see a fish rising to what appear to be invisible insects, there are three possibilities:

1. The fish is eating tiny, dark insects that are too small to see from your vantage point. Try a small, dark fly.

2. The fish is eating insects that ride low in the surface film. These could be spent mayfly spinners, egg-laying caddisflies, ants, or beetles. If it's evening, try a size 16 Rusty Spinner (this fly imitates a ton of mayfly spinners and is a good bet anywhere in the country). If it's during the day, try a size 18 ant or size 14 beetle.

3. The fish is eating emerging insects just under the surface. If you don't see any bubbles along with the rise form, this is often the case. Fish an emerger, or don't false cast your dry fly so it drifts just under the surface.

58

How does water temperature affect trout fishing?

TROUT ARE COLD-BLOODED AND MOST ACTIVE AT WATER temperatures between 55 and 65 degrees Fahrenheit Within this temperature range, they'll feed actively, rise to the surface readily for dry flies, take nymphs aggressively, and chase streamers for six feet or more. Below 50 degrees, trout feed less often because their metabolism slows down, and as a result they won't move very far for a fly. They'll also migrate to slower, deeper pools in very cold water, so the best way to fish for trout in cold water is with a nymph fished slowly, close to the bottom.

From 65 to 74 degrees trout don't feed as readily. At these temperatures their metabolism stays high but the ability of the warmer water to hold enough dissolved oxygen to sustain them is greatly decreased, because colder water can hold more dissolved oxygen. Sustained feeding at these temperatures exhausts them—in fact, catch-and-release anglers normally stop fishing at these temperatures because playing a fish when water temperatures are in the 70s can tire a fish to the point where it can't be revived. Sustained temperatures above 74 degrees will kill trout, although they can tolerate temperatures into the high 70s for short periods, as long as they aren't stressed and temperatures during the night fall back into the 60s.

If the temperature in a river approaches the high 60s in the middle of the day, the best fishing will be early in the morning, when water temperatures are at a minimum. It's often thought that evening fishing in hot weather is equally productive, but most rivers stay warm until after midnight because water cools more slowly than the surrounding land.

◀ In cold water, trout will not move very far for a fly, so slow and deep is the strategy.

59

How does weather affect trout fishing?

I'M NOT A BIG BELIEVER IN THE EFFECTS OF A BAROMETER change on trout fishing, because a fish rising from the bottom of two feet of water to the surface experiences pressure changes far exceeding those due to atmospheric pressure, so I just can't see why a change in the barometer should affect the behavior of fish. However, I *am* a big believer in the effect of light levels and wind, and a change in barometer typically accompanies a change in cloud cover and the wind speed and direction.

Trout will feed in bright sunlight, and will feed actively if the sunny weather stimulates a hatch of insects, which often occurs in spring when water temperatures are low and sun on the water warms it enough to induce insects to hatch. However, most insects are programmed to hatch during low light levels because their greatest threats are from birds and from desiccation. Birds are less active in low light and the chances of a hatching insect drying out are much lower when it's cloudy, so often when a sudden storm darkens the sky, you'll see an abundant hatch of insects and heavy feeding by trout.

I'm really not sure why windy days inhibit trout feeding, but they seem to. In my experience, the worst weather for trout fishing is just after a cold front has passed, as the bright sunlight, lower water temperatures, and wind just seem to put the fish off. Given a choice, my favorite weather for trout fishing is a calm, cloudy, humid day. A slight drizzle doesn't hurt, either. Pack your rain jacket and enjoy the great fishing.

60

How fast should you gather line when fishing upstream?

FISHING UPSTREAM IS VERY EFFECTIVE WHEN FISHING A dry fly or nymph, but is tiring because you must gather the line in front of your rod tip constantly. Usually when fishing upstream you're trying to make your fly drift naturally with the current, so you should gather line just as fast as the current brings it back to you—not so fast that you pull the fly, but fast enough that slack line does not gather under the tip of your rod. Slack line under the rod tip makes it difficult to set the hook, and it also makes it difficult to pick up line when you need to make a new cast.

When fishing upstream, gather the line as the current brings it back to you.

61

How much do you need to learn about insects?

THE THOUGHT OF LEARNING ENTOMOLOGY SCARES
many would-be fly fishers as it dredges up memories of high-school science
class. Is it helpful to learn a little basic aquatic entomology? Absolutely,
because different groups of aquatic insects have different life histories and
different behavior, and knowing, for instance, that most stoneflies crawl to
the shallows to hatch and don't ride the current when hatching might save
you from needlessly fishing a stonefly dry fly, even if you see a lot of them
in the air.

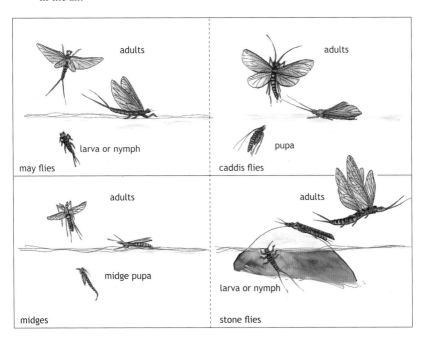

As you learn about these insects, you naturally learn more about their life history, and when you understand the behavior of trout *prey* as well as trout, you'll develop a canny instinct for predicting what the fish will do next. My advice is to learn at least to identify the four most important orders of insects and then learn a little about their life histories. These four orders are mayflies, caddisflies, stoneflies, and midges. Learning to identify the adults in the air and the larvae when you turn over rocks in a river is not hard and may even add to your enjoyment and appreciation of all aquatic life.

- Mayflies fly slowly after they hatch and look like sailboats on the water and tiny butterflies in the air. The nymphs have threadlike gills along the abdomen.

- Caddisflies skip and bounce on the water when hatching and look like moths in the air. Most caddis larvae build cases of stones and sticks, although some common species don't build cases. These "free-living" larvae usually look like green or tan grubs. All caddisflies have a brief pupa stage between the larva and adult stages that is not often seen but is very important to trout.

- Stoneflies are clumsy fliers in the air, and two pairs of wings are visible as they fly. The nymphs are flat with thick legs and tails, and crawl onto rocks along the shore to hatch.

- Midges are tiny insects with only one pair of wings and look like gnats in the air and on the water. The larvae look like tiny worms and are often bright red or green. Like caddisflies, they have a brief pupa stage and the pupae are typically dark brown or black and very appealing to trout.

How to decide
what nymph to use

IT'S PRETTY EASY TO FIGURE OUT WHAT FLY TO USE WHEN fish are rising because you often observe what insect the fish are eating. However, if you suspect trout are feeding underwater on nymphs, the clues aren't so obvious. One of the first things to do is to turn over some rocks to see what kind of aquatic insects are present. The best rocks to check are flat ones in riffled water because these are more hospitable for larvae. Many nymphs migrate to the shallows before hatching, so check the rocks closest to shore. Better yet, carry a small aquarium net and stir up a small bit of gravel and stones with your feet, holding the net just downstream to pick up the animals that get dislodged. The reason this is better than just turning over rocks is that some insects bury themselves in the gravel or silt and don't live on the underside of rocks, and seining in this way may turn up crustaceans like crayfish or baitfish like sculpins.

Now it's a simple matter to poke through your fly box for a fly that is about the same size and color as one of the critters you've dislodged. The most abundant one is your best bet, even if it isn't the biggest, juiciest one you see. If that doesn't work, try an imitation of the next most abundant creature.

If all else fails, just try some of the most popular artificial nymphs until you find one that works. Over the years, flies get popular because they work well in trout waters throughout the world, as the insects from a trout stream in New Zealand are not that different from the bugs in a California mountain stream. You can't go wrong with a size 14 Beadhead Hare's Ear, a size 12 Prince Nymph, or a size 18 Pheasant Tail Nymph. One of those will work most days in any trout stream in the world.

If a little olive mayfly nymph is the most common one you see when sampling the stream bed, choose your imitation accordingly.

How do you fish for trout in very small streams?

TROUT DON'T NEED MUCH WATER, AND IT'S AMAZING how many can be in a tiny stream that you can barely jump across. The little trickles are often overlooked by most anglers, but you can have lots of fun plucking colorful little jewels from tiny streams. Trout in small streams are usually not very picky about what they eat, but are very spooky. So the fly pattern you choose is nowhere near as critical as your approach. Work upstream so you sneak up on fish in their blind spots, and keep your profile low by kneeling or at least crouching. Short casts, obviously, are mandatory, not only because you may not have much back-cast room but also because most of the pools you fish will be tiny and you may only get a foot or two of drift before you have to pick up for another cast.

The most effective way to fish small streams is with a dry fly. The fish lie shallow and can see your dry fly even if they are lying on the bottom, and small streams don't produce as many aquatic insects as bigger rivers, so trout in the smaller waters rely a lot more on terrestrial insects that fall into the water—perfectly imitated by your fly coming from above. Choose a dry fly that floats high and that you can see, because trout in small streams take a fly quickly and you need to watch your fly so you don't miss any strikes. It's hard to beat a Royal Wulff, Stimulator, or Parachute Adams, all of which are highly visible and good floaters.

Keeping a low profile and fishing straight upstream will help you approach spooky trout in small streams.

What to do when you can't see your dry fly

IT'S IMPORTANT TO BE ABLE TO TRACK YOUR DRY FLY'S float down the current, and not only so you can see when a trout takes it. Just as important is to make sure that your fly is floating alongside that midstream rock, or over a rising fish, or that your fly is not dragging unnaturally in the current. Accuracy is more important with dries than with any other type of fly, but once your fly lands on the water it might do things you wouldn't expect because of conflicting currents.

First, it's important that you see where your fly lands so you can pick it up quickly. A few false casts over your target will give you a good idea of where the fly will land. Second, try to get in good light. Sometimes just a slight change in position will give you a better view of your fly. I often find that removing my polarized sunglasses actually helps track a dry fly if the light is dull, because glare sometimes helps you pick out your fly better against the shiny surface. If you can, change to a fly with white upright wings like a Parachute Adams or Parachute Hare's Ear. Actually, any parachute fly will be easier to see because the wings stick up plainly.

If those tricks fail, you still have a few more. Treating the fly with silicone desiccant powder, the stuff used to re-float a drowned fly, helps it stand out better against the surface. Not only does the powder make the fly float higher, it brightens the fly a little and keeps it visible. If you are convinced you need a small, dark fly or a low-floating fly, both types that are tricky to see even under the best lighting, make your small fly a dropper. Tie on a large, high-floating dry fly you can see, and then tie about twenty inches of tippet to the bend of the big fly and add your little one behind it. Now you can watch the big fly, knowing that if the big fly drags the little fly will, too. And if you see a rise anywhere near the big fly—or if it goes under—set the hook!

The white parachute wing on this Royal PMX helps you track it on the water. ▶

65

Preparing for your first float trip

CHANCES ARE YOUR FIRST GUIDED TROUT-FISHING TRIP will be in a drift boat with a friend or guide. With a little preparation, you'll have a lot more fun and keep the stress level for both you and your guide to a minimum.

- Be honest with your ability so the guide can plan a day on water that suits your experience level. He'll figure it out in five minutes anyway if you exaggerate.
- Most guides provide lunch, equipment, and flies—but some don't. Make sure you establish that the guide is bringing lunch and drinks before you're five miles into a ten-mile trip on a hot day.
- Don't wear wading shoes with metal cleats. They'll tear up the bottom of the guide's expensive boat. If they're the only wading boots you own, wear a pair of sandals or sneakers and only put on the wading boots if you get out and wade while on the trip.
- The guide will give you directions based on the hands of a clock. Twelve o'clock is not whatever is in front of you. It's always the front of the boat, and six o'clock is directly behind the boat.
- Pack a raincoat and try to get all your gear into one bag that can be easily stowed.
- It's best to fish and move around the boat as directed by the guide. If you want to try a cast in a different spot, ask first so you don't risk hooking the guide or falling out of the boat when you suddenly do something he didn't expect.

Evening Shadows

66

Reading currents
to find trout

BEHAVIORAL STUDIES OF TROUT HAVE SHOWN THAT THEY prefer current speeds of about ten to twelve inches per second, which is about the speed of a slow walk. Try pacing it out with your foot. However, while they like to lie in water of this speed, they also like to be on the edge of a faster current, because the faster the current, the quicker food is brought to them. Thus the best place to find trout is where fast currents meet slower water, known as a seam. You can see these obvious breaks on the edges of fast surface currents, but there are also hidden seams below the surface.

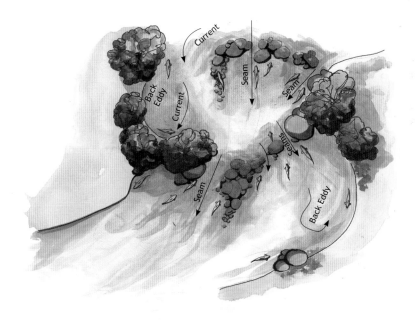

Hidden seams are found on stream bottoms with rough texture, because each rock on the bottom makes turbulence and slows the downstream progress of currents. Thus, a piece of water studded with large boulders will hold more trout than one with a smooth sand or gravel bottom. The friction of water running along a bank creates a seam as well, and here, too, a bank with a rough or uneven shoreline will hold more trout than a smooth bank where the current runs swift and unbroken.

This angler is fishing to the other side of a distinct seam where fast water meets slower current.

Changes in depth also create hidden seams. Any place deep water meets shallow will be likely to hold feeding trout, as long as the shallow side is at least eight inches deep. Trout will feed in surprisingly shallow water if not disturbed, and if threatened they can quickly dart back into the depths to hide.

67

Setting the hook on trout

THE HOOKS USED IN MOST TROUT FLIES ARE SMALL AND very sharp. Trout jaws are almost the perfect medium for sinking a hook, and if you have trouble setting the hook, the problem could be your reflexes—but it could also be the fish. Trout quickly detect the fraud in our flies, and unlike when caught with bait, they eject a fly in a flash. If you don't set the hook the moment a trout takes your fly, you'll miss the opportunity. They won't wait around gumming your fly until you get your act together. Striking to a trout is simple—just raise your rod tip enough to take all of the slack out of your line and tighten the line until you feel resistance—no more, or you can risk breaking the tippet.

If you keep missing fish and are sure you're striking quickly enough, it may be the trout and not you. A trout that moves to a dry fly but changes its mind at the last minute because it doesn't like the fly or sees it suddenly begin to drag still has forward momentum and can't put on the brakes quickly enough. What happens is that the trout splashes at your fly with its mouth closed. We call this a refusal, and it means you were close but not close enough. Change your casting angle to avoid drag or try a fly one size smaller if you think you are getting refusals.

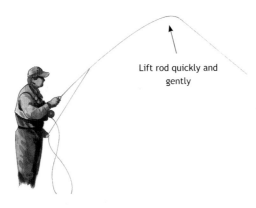

Lift rod quickly and gently

Trout also chase streamers, and sometimes seem only to want to move that obnoxious, gaudy thing out of their territory. They sometimes just bump the fly or even throw a cross-body block at it without connecting. Try fishing the same fly slower or faster, which seems to be more productive than changing flies.

Setting the hook on trout is a matter of just lifting the tip of the rod enough to tighten the line.

What do you do if a rising trout won't take your fly?

YOU'VE FINALLY FOUND A STEADILY RISING TROUT, AND despite your best efforts, you can't get it to take your fly. Congratulations! At least you have not spooked the fish, and that's more than half the battle. Many anglers prefer trout that are tough to catch on a dry fly because they love the challenge of matching wits with an animal whose brain is smaller than your thumbnail.

More than half the time, a trout will refuse your fly not because the fly was wrong but because it was not behaving naturally. Because your fly is connected to a line and leader that drift at different speeds than the fly, and often land in currents of different velocities, it's very difficult to get a float free of drag for very long. Sometimes just a change in position will give you a longer float. A longer, lighter tippet can also help—if your tippet is twenty-four inches of 5X, try thirty inches of 6X instead. You can also try casting a lot of slack, which will prolong the natural drift of your fly before drag sets in.

If you're sure that your presentation is good, then it's time to try a new fly. I've found that the best approach is to try a fly one size smaller with a slightly different profile. For example, if you see the fish taking what looks like a size 16 cream-colored mayfly and you've been fishing with a size 16 Pale Evening Dun, try a size 18 Sparkle Dun. And if that doesn't work, the fish may be taking the emerging mayflies just under the surface, so try a cream-colored emerger.

If a fish keeps rising but ignores your fly, often a smaller imitation will do the trick.

What do you do if the water is dirty?

REALLY FILTHY WATER THE COLOR OF COFFEE WITH cream, with visibility of less than a couple inches and lots of debris floating down a river, usually means you should read a book or head to the nearest establishment that serves fine food and drink. Sometimes, if you catch rising water when it first begins to get dirty a streamer will draw very aggressive strikes from fish that are on the prowl for disoriented baitfish, but once the water has been dirty for over an hour it's going to be slim pickings and I really can't offer you much solace.

However, dirty water with visibility of ten inches or more can actually work in your favor, because trout lose a lot of their caution when they can't see out of the water very well. In this situation, look for trout in slower, shallower water where they can still find food in the slower, less turbulent current of a still pool. Dry flies, nymphs, and streamers all work well in slightly dirty water, especially if it is in that optimum temperature range of 55 to 65 degrees farenheit.

In dirty water, a big streamer may be the only fly a trout can see.

What do you do
if you don't see any trout?

TAKE HEART. JUST BECAUSE YOU DON'T SEE ANY TROUT in the water does not mean a river is lifeless. Unless trout are obviously feeding on the surface, you may not see any, because they are very well camouflaged; otherwise, they would not survive. The best place to see trout in a river is from a high vantage point where you can creep up to the edge without spooking them, but even in perfectly clear water you can stare at the bottom for many minutes before you finally pick up the shape of a tail or a shadow that moves sideways. In some rivers, trout are relatively easy to spot, but in most you can fish all day long (and catch a dozen) without ever seeing one in the water. If you know the water holds trout, fish a streamer or a nymph over places you think will hold fish.

If you don't see any trout in the water, take heart. Even from a good vantage point looking down into the water, this brown trout (in the center of the photo) is so well-camoflauged it is nearly invisible.

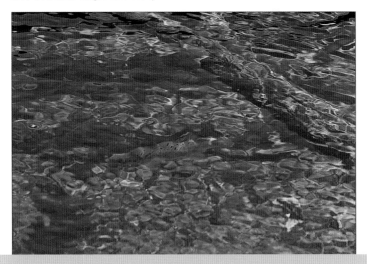

71

What do you do when you scare all the fish?

TROUT ARE VERY GOOD AT SEEING US, AND WE'RE PRETTY big and clumsy critters in their world. You will scare fish. In fact, I believe that even the best fly fishers scare over half of the fish in a pool before ever getting a cast over them. You probably won't see many trout bolting for cover in fright, either, because they are good at sneaking away before you can spot them, unless the water is very low and clear and the sun is directly overhead.

You may *suspect* that you're scaring fish when you never seem to catch any, and this is especially common in small streams, where the fish aren't terribly picky about flies but are very wary of predators. There are many tricks to help you fish without scaring the fish.

Skinny Water

- Fish can see out of the water, and the deeper they are the better they can see you. They do have a blind spot directly behind them, so working upstream helps. Just be careful of fish in whirlpools, as some of them may be facing downstream.

- Keeping your profile low is especially important when not fishing upstream. Objects close to the ground or surface of the water are tougher for a trout to spot.

- Objects that move are immediately spotted by all animals. Try to keep your movements slow, and keep a high bank or trees behind you so your silhouette does not stand out against the sky.

- Fish can't see very well into the sun but are very frightened by sudden shadows on the water. Try to keep the sun at your back but avoid letting your shadow fall on the water.

- Fish are equally sensitive to vibrations, which travel a long way underwater. Tread lightly on the bank, try not to roll rocks with your feet as you wade, and don't slap your fly line on the water.

- When fishing in a still pool, don't create a wake when you wade. Sudden waves across the still surface of a pool can send every trout within fifty yards bolting for cover. This sometimes means moving excruciatingly slowly, but it will be worth the effort.

72

What is a mend and when should you do it?

IN MOST DRY FLY AND NYMPH FISHING, THE BEST presentation is a dead drift, which means the fly moves at exactly the same speed as the current, no slower and no faster. When swinging a wet fly in the current for steelhead, salmon, or trout, the best presentation is usually obtained by having the fly line in a straight line as it swings in the current. And when fishing a sinking-tip fly line, it's important to keep the floating portion of your line from pulling on the weighted part because the floater will draw the sinking part back to the surface. Forty feet of fly line cast across several different currents never behaves the way you want it to, and this is where mends come in handy.

Making a mend is easier than deciding when and where to use one. If you make a cast straight across a uniform current, you'll see that the line in

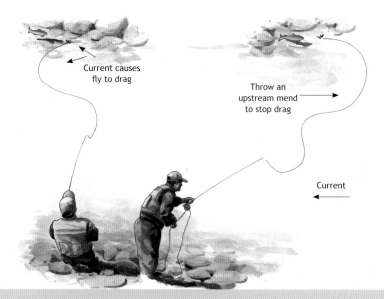

Current causes fly to drag

Throw an upstream mend to stop drag

Current

the middle of the cast begins to move downstream faster than the line that is held close the rod tip, and faster than the fly and leader, which are slowed down by resistance to the water. As a result, as the line swings round, the fly begins to accelerate like the end of a whip. A little acceleration at the end of a swing is sometimes desirable, but left unattended it's too abrupt to appeal to most fish. By reaching out with the rod and making a quick flip upstream, you can straighten the fly line, or actually move the arc upstream in a mirror image of itself, depending on how much you want the swing to slow down or how deep you want your sinking-tip fly line to descend.

There may be times when you want a downstream mend, especially when your fly lands in fast water and the current between you and the fly is slower. In this case you mend in the opposite, downstream direction. Mends can be done with a stiff arm, a quick flip of the wrist, or a combination of the two. The more line you have to mend, the longer your rod should reach and the higher you'll have to reach with the rod. It doesn't matter how you do it as long as you move the line without moving the fly.

73

What is an emerger fly and when should you use one?

A NATURAL EMERGER IS AN AQUATIC INSECT AT THE moment it reaches the meniscus. The surface is quite a barrier to emerging flies, and they often struggle against it, more helpless than they are at any other time in their short life spans. Trout recognize this easy meal and go out of their way to prey on emergers. If you see trout rising but they keep refusing your dry flies or seem to be swirling in the current without breaking the surface, they may be taking emergers.

An emerger fly is a dry fly that doesn't float well or a nymph that doesn't sink. Take your pick on the definition. Emergers are tied with light wire hooks but with materials that don't float well, so they hang just below the surface or right in the film. Sometimes a bit of fly floatant helps keep them suspended, but often just a few false casts will keep them right where they should be. Fish an emerger just like you would a dry fly, and strike to the rise the same way you would a dry, because even if a trout takes your fly just under the surface it will still produce a swirl when it eats.

Emerger flies float right in the surface film.

74

When is the best time of day to go trout fishing?

THE BEST TIME TO GO FISHING FOR TROUT IS WHEN their food is active. It's typically also the most pleasant time of day for humans. So in winter and through the beginning of May at lower altitudes and through June at higher altitudes, the best time to go fishing is in the middle of the day, when the water warms up enough to stimulate insect hatches and get a trout's metabolism moving. As summer progresses and the weather gets hotter in the middle of the day, the best time to go trout fishing is at dawn and dusk. In fall it reverts back to mid-day.

There are a few caveats to this rule. Dawn and dusk are nearly always worth trying, unless the water is below 50 degrees, because although insects may not be hatching, trout may be prowling the shallows for minnows and crustaceans when light levels are low. Also, late morning through late afternoon can be good for trout fishing as long as the water does not rise above 65 degrees, because ants, beetles, grasshoppers, and other land insects are more active in the hot parts of the day and fall into the water, especially on windy days.

And, of course, the answer you'll get from many authorities on the best time to go trout fishing is, "When you can get away."

In the warmer days of the season, dawn and dusk are the best times for trout fishing. ▶

75

When to fish streamers

THERE IS SOMETIMES ONE STREAMER PATTERN THAT out-fishes others, and frequently the speed you strip line when fishing a streamer is important. But I've found that it's more a matter of timing and location in a river, and when trout are really pounding streamers it's hard not to catch them. First, streamers are always productive when the light is low, when predatory trout have an advantage over the faster, more maneuverable baitfish. Dawn, dusk, after dark, and during rainstorms are the best times to catch trout on streamers.

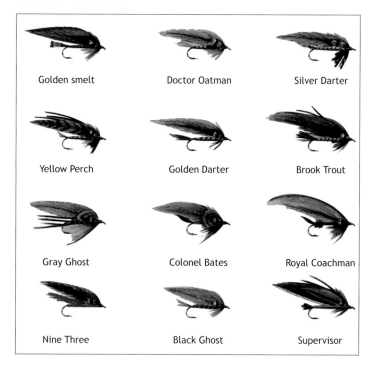

Golden smelt	Doctor Oatman	Silver Darter
Yellow Perch	Golden Darter	Brook Trout
Gray Ghost	Colonel Bates	Royal Coachman
Nine Three	Black Ghost	Supervisor

Water temperatures in the prime range for trout, 55 to 65 degrees, also make them more aggressive for streamers, because a trout will often chase a streamer eight to ten feet before grabbing it, and they just won't move that far for a fly when the water is too cold or too warm. Water that is just starting to get dirty after a sudden rainstorm is one of the best times, as dirty water disorients baitfish and trout will begin feeding on baitfish like someone threw a bucket of chum in the water.

Trout can be caught on streamers in the middle of a bright, sunny day. It seems like about 5 percent of the trout in any given stretch of water can be induced to chase a streamer in bright sunlight, and this is why fishing streamers from a drift boat is so productive—you cover so much water that you're bound to put your fly over one of those takers. The best places to catch fish on streamers in the middle of the day are stretches of fast, heavy water and deep water around logs and big jumbles of rocks, where large trout wait in ambush.

76

Where will you find trout in a lake?

WHEN FACED WITH A FLAT EXPANSE OF WATER WITH NO current, even experienced fly fishers panic. Lakes are not as easy to read as rivers, trout can be anywhere because there are no currents to keep them pinioned to one spot, and in lakes you have both geography and depth to worry about. Local knowledge is best, but there are a few tips that can help you narrow down the possibilities.

- Scan the lake surface with binoculars for rising fish early in the morning or right before dark. Chances are any trout that are hungry will come to the surface then looking for hatching insects.
- Inlets and outlets are always hotspots in lakes. Trout spawn in moving water in spring and fall, and inlets bring in hatches of insects.
- In the cold water of early and late season, look for trout in shallows where the water is warmer than the depths.
- Springs coming into a lake will attract trout in both cold and warm water, as springs are warmer than lake water in the early spring and colder during the summer. If springs aren't obvious, put a thermometer on a long string and take temperatures close to the bottom at various places.
- Submerged weed beds hold more insect life than sand or rock bottoms, so look for trout close to aquatic vegetation.

◀ *On Secret Pond*

Warmwater Fly Fishing

77

Flies to use for smallmouth bass in rivers

SMALLMOUTH BASS EAT INSECTS AND BAITFISH JUST LIKE trout, and you can fish for them with your standard trout flies. But that's not as effective and certainly not as much fun as getting them to chase bigger bugs. A smallmouth's number one prey is crayfish; thus any streamer with lots of action and stuff wiggling at all angles to look like the claws and legs of a crayfish will drive them wild. Bead-Head Woolly Buggers with rubber legs, Yellow Muddler Minnows, and patterns with rabbit strips all appeal to smallmouths. Throw in a few patterns that look more like a baitfish, such as a Clouser Minnow or a White Zonker, and you'll have the streamers covered.

The Woolly Bugger is one of the best flies for river smallmouths.

Another favorite smallmouth food is the hellgrammite, a large black larva of the dobsonfly. A black Woolly Bugger or large black stonefly nymph with rubber legs will do for them. Fish these dead drift, with or without a strike indicator, especially on days when smallmouths aren't aggressive and inclined to chase streamers.

Don't rule out surface poppers, though. Smallmouths will investigate small bass bugs, often hanging back for a full minute before smashing them, but there is nothing more thrilling than catching a frisky smallmouth bass on a bug. Even if you come upon a smallmouth sipping delicate mayflies on the surface, you can often convince it to go for a bigger mouthful and inhale a bass bug that is ten times the size of the mayflies it's eating. And there is no better surface bug for smallmouths than the cone-shaped chartreuse popper with rubber legs known as a Sneaky Pete.

Smallmouth Bass

78

How to find a bass and panfish pond close to home

IT'S SILLY TO WAIT FOR A TRIP TO MONTANA OR ALASKA to enjoy some fly fishing. Anglers who have fished throughout the world still thrill to the dawn rise of a largemouth bass to a popper in a suburban golf course pond. And the many species of sunfish swirl eagerly to small poppers and regulation trout flies, making you feel like a hero. I would be willing to bet there is a pond within five miles of your house that holds some bass and

Chances are you won't have to travel far to find a pond filled with bass or sunfish.

panfish, no matter where you live. Even the ponds in Central Park are packed with eager bass and panfish just waiting to inhale a fly.

Here's how to find one: Pick the pond closest to your house that is *reasonably* accessible. ("No fishing" signs on golf course ponds are only meant to be obeyed during the day, and dawn raids on these places will evoke thrills you forgot when you reached puberty.) When spring flowers begin to bloom (this might be March in Florida or May in North Dakota), begin scouting the shoreline for saucer-shaped nests made by bass and panfish as they clean a place on the bottom prior to laying eggs. The spots typically show up as a light spot or a clean area of gravel in an otherwise muddy bottom. Now you know fish live there. Catching them is simply a matter of trying a small surface bug or a size 10 Hare's Ear Nymph.

After spawning is over in a few weeks, the fish will stay close to the shallows, but in midsummer they might spend most of their time deeper, in the middle of the pond. But don't worry. They still come close to shore to feed at dawn and dusk, when you can sneak in without getting caught.

Small Fry – Largemouth Bass

79

How to find bass in a pond or lake

YOU *CAN* CATCH LARGEMOUTH AND SMALLMOUTH BASS anywhere the Bassmaster folks can catch them with conventional tackle, but you probably won't bother, because catching bass with a fly sometimes involves fishing a sinking line in twenty feet of water. Most of us prefer to catch our bass on the surface or close to it, where we can fish a floating line. Casting and picking up a floating line is a pleasure instead of a chore. Bass ambush their prey, so when fishing for them in shallow water you will seldom find them far from dense weed beds, logjams, piles of big rocks, or docks. Largemouths prefer dense mats of lily pads, cattails, and other aquatic weeds, and they will be *in* the weeds, not just close to them. A weedless fly helps. Sometimes they won't move more than a few inches from their ambush point, so you should cast right into the nasty stuff. Smallmouths prefer rocky bottoms. Look for them close to submerged logs and large boulders, especially close to a place where shallow water quickly drops off into the depths.

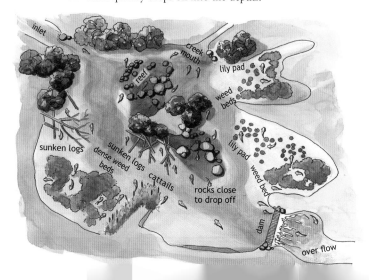

How to fish a bass bug

WHETHER FISHING FOR LARGEMOUTH BASS, SMALLMOUTH bass, or sunfish, you should begin by fishing a surface bug slowly. Slow enough that you get impatient. Bass are infinitely more patient than you. The natural tendency is to cast the bug and begin moving it as soon as it hits the water, like something trying to get away. Bass prefer prey that is struggling, and most animals that struggle twitch a few times, then rest motionless.

So cast your bug and don't move it. Strip in enough line to come tight to the fly but not enough to move it. Then wait until all the rings around the fly disappear. Don't worry about a bass losing interest, as they often approach potential prey and eyeball it for a full minute before making a decision. Time and again, a bass will wait until everything gets quiet and then suddenly pounce on a fly that is totally motionless. After you've waited so long you can't stand it, give the fly a single twitch. Move it about an inch. Then wait again. Continue this way until the fly is close enough to pick up for another cast.

This twitch-and-wait strategy is by far the most productive way to fish a bug, but if it doesn't work, by all means try others. If the water is deep, sometimes three or four abrupt twitches followed by a long pause bring bass up from deeper water when they hear the commotion. You can also try a steady retrieve, where you keep the fly moving and never let it pause. Experiment until you find the right formula, and it will work for you throughout the day.

A deer hair mouse and a cork popper, two very popular bugs for largemouth bass

How to fish a bass streamer

LARGEMOUTH BASS SELDOM CHASE A FLY AGGRESSIVELY as they are ambushers—sprinters, and not long-distance runners. When you fish a sinking bass fly, move it slowly and steadily, and when presenting a subsurface fly to bass try to position your cast so that nearly your entire retrieve moves the fly along near cover. In other words, if a big log sticks out into a lakeshore, don't make a cast at 90 degrees to the log, because only the first foot or so of your retrieve will be appealing to bass lying in ambush. Instead, position yourself so that your fly will swim along parallel to the log, presenting a tasty morsel to a lurking bass throughout its progress.

Get that streamer in the middle of the thick stuff, too, not just along the edges. Cast your streamer right into the lily pads, drawing it over the surface of the pads, letting it sink into the holes between them. Even with a weed-less fly you'll get frequent snags, but if your fly is not in deep cover it won't be fishing where largemouths feed.

Smallmouth bass are found more often amongst rocks and logs than weeds, so here you should try to fish your fly so that it rides just above piles of large rocks on the bottom, or off rocky points and cliffs. A weighted fly like a Clouser Minnow is deadly on smallmouths, and these heavy flies should be fished with a strip and then a pause that lets the fly sink. Smallmouths usually pounce on a fly that is sinking or just beginning to rise after it has sunk, so watch your line for any twitch or pause because a big smallmouth may have just inhaled your fly.

Typical subsurface streamers used for bass

Picking the right leader for warmwater fly fishing

BASS ARE NOT LEADER-SHY, AND EVEN A FLY LINE LANDING on top of one seldom spooks it. For largemouth bass, the leader should be as heavy as you can find, and if you can get the leader through the eye of the fly you've gone as light as you need to. Big bass flies are very wind-resistant, and a short, stiff leader helps turn them over, so a leader of between six and seven and a half feet long with a breaking strength of fifteen to twenty pounds is about right. You'll appreciate that heavy leader when yanking a big largemouth out of aquatic salad, too. Smallmouths live in clear water and are slightly spookier than largemouths, so a nine-foot leader that breaks at twelve pounds will straighten the smaller flies used for them and will land even a world-record smallmouth with ease.

Musky Moon

When and how to catch carp on a fly

CARP CAN THRIVE IN ALL KINDS OF WATERS, FROM LARGER trout streams to the most polluted urban lakes. Although some consider them to be pests, carp are highly prized in Asian and European countries and were originally introduced into North America as a food fish. Fly fishers have discovered that carp are stronger fighters than many celebrated gamefish, and are just as difficult to catch as a spring creek trout or a tropical permit.

Carp are best on a fly rod in spring, when they cruise shallow water to seek warmth, look for mates, and lay eggs. Fishing for carp in deeper water where they can't be spotted is nearly fruitless, because a successful presentation must put the fly right in front of a carp's nose. Carp cannot see very well and find much of their food by smell, but they will pounce on an object moving just a few inches away that looks like a crayfish, insect larva,

Mirror carp

or minnow. However, just because they can't see well does not mean they are easy to approach. Carp are extremely cautious of vibrations in the water, so sloppy wading, noise from a boat, or the splash of a fly line landing close is a sure way to send a school of them dashing for cover.

Look for carp in shallow water with a silt or sand bottom, along the edges of weeds. If present, they'll give themselves away by rolling, waking, and even jumping clear of the water. Try to determine which way a fish is moving and throw a weighted nymph or small streamer two to three feet ahead of the fish so that the sound of the fly and line hitting the water don't spook the fish. When you think the fish is close to your fly, begin moving it slowly and steadily, close to the bottom, like a crayfish or insect larva that has been dislodged by the rooting carp and is trying to get away. If you feel resistance, set the hook with a long and brisk strip rather than lifting your rod, because if you miss the fish it might follow the fly and give you a second chance.

Don't be discouraged if you spook many of the fish and if they ignore your fly. Carp may not be pretty and glamorous, but they are some of the smartest, most wary fish in fresh water. The fact that they are so abundant gives you plenty of opportunities to try again!

84

Where to find smallmouth bass in a river

BECAUSE SMALLMOUTH BASS ARE NOT AS STREAMLINED AS trout and will pursue and ambush their prey as opposed to lying in the current waiting for food to drift by, they are commonly found in slower water than trout. Look for smallmouths in deep eddies at the heads of pools, in rock piles at the tails of pools, and halfway down large pools, along the deeper bank especially if it is lined with ledge rock, big boulders, or fallen logs. Smallmouths will also lie on the outside edges of weed beds in large, warm rivers, waiting to ambush baitfish that use the weeds for protection.

◀ Smallmouth bass prefer rocky streams and lakes.

VIII

Saltwater Fly Fishing

85

How do you catch fish on a fly in the surf?

FLY FISHING IN CRASHING SURF SEEMS AT FIRST TO BE A daunting prospect, but many saltwater gamefish like striped bass, bluefish, sea trout, surf perch, and corbina prey on baitfish and crustaceans that get disoriented and corralled along the shoreline in rough weather. The most important aspect of surf fishing is line control. Tony Stetzko, known as "Striperman" on Cape Cod, specializes in fly fishing the big surf along the National Seashore, and taught me to take a cast and then take three steps backward. You must come tight to your line quickly when fishing the surf; otherwise, the incoming waves put too much slack in your line. Sinking

When fishing the surf, line control is important. Wearing a stripping basket and taking three steps back after every cast will help.

or intermediate weight lines are usually best in the surf. By getting just below the surface currents, you'll retain a better connection to your fly as the sinking line somewhat counteracts surface turbulence.

The best presentation in the waves is to wait for a big wave to break, and then cast your line as far as you can beyond the wave in the slick behind it. This will give you an expanse of relatively calm water to strip your fly through, ensuring that the fish see it better and that your line does not get pushed around by too many waves. Don't always cast directly into the waves. The tide will usually be moving one direction or another along the beach, so try some casts both "down-tide" and "up-tide" so that your fly runs parallel to the beach, which mimics the behavior of baitfish.

A stripping basket is essential when fishing the surf. You often need to strip line quickly, and if you strip line at your feet it will swirl around your legs and tangle in them, and will also pick up bits of weed and debris. A stripping basket keeps fly line coiled and ready for the next cast.

Finally, when landing a big fish in the surf, play it close to the surf line and then hold it in place until the next big wave. Just before a big wave breaks over the fish, walk backward quickly and use the power of the wave to roll your fish up onto the beach, where it will be left sideways in shallow water, ready for you to dash to it before the next big wave breaks. And when admiring your fish or holding it up for others to see, remember—never turn your back to a wave!

86

Which tide is best for saltwater fly fishing?

THERE IS NO "BEST" TIDE FOR SALTWATER FLY FISHING, AS the right tide to fish varies with each location. When fishing beaches or estuaries, the first stage of the tide, when water reverses direction and begins to move, is usually best, but I know of some places when the last hour of an incoming or outgoing tide offers the best fishing.

In general, an outgoing tide is best on the outside of an estuary or tidal marsh, where it hits bigger water, because baitfish and crustaceans from the food-rich shallows get washed into deeper water, where bigger fish lie in ambush. On an incoming tide, fish move with the rising water back inside estuaries when more water allows them to cruise food-rich areas, so on a rising tide you may find more gamefish up inside a tidal marsh or salt pond.

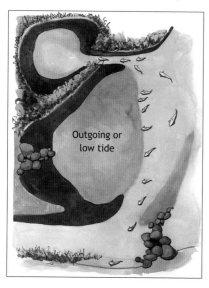

Outgoing or low tide

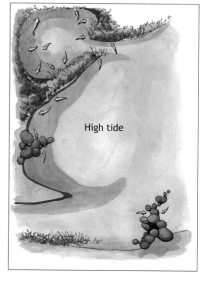

High tide

Estuary

On most shallow sand and coral flats the best fishing is on an incoming tide. The rising water exposes productive feeding areas that have been inaccessible to the fish, as shallow water always hosts more baitfish and crustaceans than deep water. And when sight fishing on the flats, the fish are a lot easier to spot in skinny water than they are when the flat is covered with four of five feet of water. High tide is difficult for flats fishing, as the fish are not concentrated on deeper, narrower channels and can be almost anywhere, plus they're difficult to spot. The best advice at high tide is to fish very close to the shoreline or up against coral heads or in the mangroves. On a falling tide, fish don't feed as aggressively and are often just migrating back to deeper water, but if you can find the channels they use to move into the depths you may be able to induce them to feed.

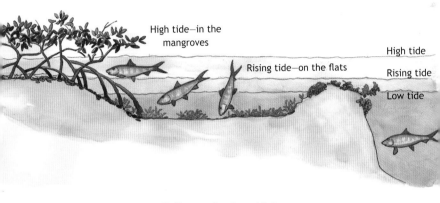

Shallow sand and coral flats

87

How to get started with redfish and sea trout on the fly

SMALL SEA TROUT AND YOUNG REDFISH OR "PUPPY DRUM" are some of the easiest fish to catch on a fly from New Jersey south to Florida on the Atlantic Coast and along the entire Gulf Coast. These fish are always hungry, relatively easy to please, and stay in shallow water throughout the season—although during strong winter cold fronts they may move to deeper holes until the water warms. Thus they are perfect fish to hone your technique and build up some confidence for saltwater fly fishing.

Both species are found in shallow water, from one to four feet deep, and are especially common over weed beds and above oyster bars. Any kind of discontinuity in the shoreline—whether a creek mouth, dock, jetty, or point—will attract them, but they can also be found along beaches on a sandy bottom. The best fly for both species is a Clouser Minnow in bright colors like chartreuse or orange, but any fly from one to three inches long that imitates baitfish, shrimp, or crabs will interest them.

Redfish and Sea Trout

Because they typically run from one to four pounds, there is a natural tendency to use a light 6- or 7-weight fly rod for small sea trout and redfish. However, the best flies for these species are weighted, and you'll often encounter wind along the shore, so if you're starting out, an 8- or even 9-weight rod is a better choice. Besides, in the fall and early winter you may encounter larger "bull" redfish of twenty or thirty pounds in the same shallow water, and if you do you'll be happy you have the heavier rod.

The most exciting fishing for redfish is on a calm, sunny day when you can spot them tailing or cruising in very shallow water. Not only is sight-fishing for them more fun, you'll learn a lot about their behavior and reaction to your fly presentations when you can see every move they make.

88

How to get started with stripers on the fly

STRIPED BASS ARE EXTREMELY COMMON ALONG THE Atlantic Coast from Maine to North Carolina and can be found as far south as Florida. They are also found in the Mississippi Delta and were introduced over one hundred years ago to the West Coast, where they are abundant in estuaries from San Francisco Bay north to Oregon. "Schoolie" stripers from eight to twenty-four inches are very common, often traveling in schools of hundreds of individuals. These juvenile striped bass are very aggressive and seldom pass up a streamer, bonefish fly, or popper. When even a sixteen-inch striped bass takes a popper, you'll think a fish three times its size has crashed your fly.

Schoolies tend to concentrate inside harbors and along beaches, often moving far inside tidal creeks and salt ponds. Look for them at the mouths of creeks, around jetties, near docks, and on shallow sandy flats, especially in early spring when they're more comfortable where the sun warms the bottom. Schools often move quickly, so you should cover a lot of water, stripping a

small weighted baitfish pattern with aggressive short, quick strips. If there are any small stripers around, they'll quickly pounce on the fly, and once you find a concentration of them, it's fun to put on a surface fly and watch them smash it.

◀ Schoolie stripers are always eager to take a fly—and they fight hard!

89

How to set the hook on bigger saltwater fish

FOR MANY SALTWATER SPECIES LIKE BONEFISH, STRIPED bass, and small redfish, a simple strip strike is enough to penetrate the jaw and secure the hook firmly. However, for large bony-jawed fish like tarpon, tuna, sailfish, trevally, redfish over twenty pounds, and even large freshwater species like pike and muskellunge, you need more force and a wider arc in your strike, plus you should strike using the butt of the rod instead of the tip. With the bigger species, strikes should be long and low. You can't do this by raising the rod tip straight in front of you because your body blocks the butt of the rod from moving past the vertical. So to strike them, jab your rod down and off to one side, using your stronger forearm and shoulder muscles instead of your wrist, which should remain locked throughout the strike. If there was any slack in the line or if you don't feel a very firm pressure when you set the hook, make another sideways jab with the rod and also make a hard strip strike by yanking the line away from the rod, just as if you were making a double haul. To be absolutely sure, some fly fishers make yet another strike after the fish has made its first run and has paused before trying its next move.

The best way to strike larger saltwater fish is to strike to the side with a low rod, sometimes using the line hand for added pressure.

90

Preparing for your first bonefishing trip

MOST PEOPLE TRAVEL A LONG WAY AND SPEND A WEEK'S PAY or more for a bonefishing trip. I've watched even experienced trout anglers get frustrated, angry, and even embarrassed on bonefishing trips because they weren't ready for the wind, difficult fish spotting, and unfamiliar directions given by a guide. Just a little preparation will make your first trip a lot more fun.

First, practice your casting. Most bonefish are caught within forty feet, but that forty-foot cast must be made quickly, under pressure, with deadly accuracy, and with the good chance of a stiff breeze. Being able to get

A Short Cast

forty feet of fly line outside the rod tip is not enough. Pace out forty feet and make sure you can hit a target the size of a hula hoop with reasonable consistency, with a wind coming from any direction, and be able to change directions to cast to another hula hoop with just one false cast. Bonefish are spooky critters and too many false casts will ruin your chances.

Either before your trip or just after you arrive, take a heavily weighted, lightly weighted, and unweighted bonefish fly to some shallow water where you can see the fly sink. Watch how fast each fly lands, as having different sink rates in bonefish flies is far more important than having the favorite fly on the island. Over sand and mud bottoms you want the fly to sink to the bottom and make little puffs of silt when you strip, because these plumes attract the attention of a bonefish looking for a crab or shrimp trying to escape. Over weedy and coral-covered bottoms, a bonefish can't see a fly that sinks down into the debris (and you'll get hung up), so you'll begin to strip your fly before it hits bottom. And you never know beforehand how deep the water will be on a given flat, so you must have some idea of how fast your fly will sink.

No matter how good you are at spotting trout or steelhead, you will have trouble seeing bonefish in the water, at least for the first day and probably for a couple days. Count on it. Bonefish are nearly invisible underwater because their shiny sides reflect the bottom, and without a shadow to pinpoint their position you'll have a very difficult time. If you are unlucky to have a week of cloudy weather you may see very few of them unless they are tailing in shallow water. Some guides are excellent at helping clients learn to spot bonefish. Others, because of a language problem or reticence, just tell their anglers where to cast and forget about trying to teach them. Try to discipline yourself to see through the water, not at it, and remember that bonefish hardly ever stop moving, so look for shadows and grayish indistinct shapes that don't stay put.

Once you get onto a boat with a guide, remember that he will be giving you directions to cast by the hands of a clock *in relation to the boat*. Twelve o'clock is always directly in front of the boat, not where you are looking. And you will get befuddled—guaranteed. I don't know how many times I've had a guide say, "Cast thirty feet at nine o'clock. *Sigh*. No. The other nine o'clock." I even saw an enterprising young Bahamian guide on my last trip who had painted the hands of the clock, including the numbers, on the bow of the boat, just for clods like me.

The other miscommunication with guides and clients is distance. Different people have different ideas of what forty feet is, especially in the heat of the moment. Make a short and a long cast before you start and ask your guide how far the casts were. If you're traveling to Mexico or Central America, it's not a bad idea to learn the Spanish words for twenty, thirty, forty, fifty, and sixty feet before you leave.

Finally, the strike is the bane of all trout anglers. You should never strike a bonefish (or any saltwater fish) with the rod tip, but by making a long, firm strip with the line while the rod is held low. Raising the rod tip lifts the fly out of the water, and if a bonefish hasn't really taken it or misses the fly, it may come back to a fly that just makes a long dart through the water rather than one that goes airborne. (Many guides, when they see a bonefish take a fly, will instruct the angler to "make a long strip" because they know if they say "strike," up will come the rod tip.) One of the best suggestions I've heard for people who cannot modify their reflexes to strip strike is to retrieve a bonefish fly with the rod tip help a few inches underwater throughout the retrieve. With the tip underwater, the line stays in excellent control and it's almost impossible to make a "trout strike."

IX

Tackle Care

Do you need to clean your gear after each trip?

MODERN FLY-FISHING TACKLE IS INCREDIBLY RESISTANT to the elements. After most fishing trips, you can put away all your gear without a care in the world. Graphite rods are totally resistant to dirt and moisture, reels are anodized to prevent corrosion and rust, and lines don't need to be dried. For nearly every piece of tackle you own, a little soap and water is all you need. Here are some tips to help keep your gear in perfect shape for many years to come:

- Your rod should not be put away in a rod tube wet, because the cloth sack can develop mildew. Just let your rod and its sack dry before putting them back in the case. Although saltwater reel seats are anodized to prevent corrosion, salt crystals can build up on a reel seat, so wash the seat with fresh water and dry before putting it away.

- Reels should also be rinsed in fresh water after a day in the salt. Some anglers strip all the line off the reel and spray some water inside to prevent salt crystals from building up on the line and backing. If any mud or grains of sand have gotten inside the reel, remove the spool and clean them with an old toothbrush. A sparse application of light machine oil on all the moving parts of a reel except the drag surfaces is a good idea several times each season.

- Lines need no maintenance besides keeping them out of the hot sun for extended periods. However, if you fish in areas with high salinity or profuse algae, it's a good idea to clean your line with soap and water after every trip.

- Waders don't need any cleaning to prolong their life, but the soles of waders should be cleaned thoroughly with hot water and soap and a scrubbing brush whenever you move from one watershed to another. Then dry the soles and inspect them for any debris. Spores and eggs of invasive species like didymo algae, mud snail, whirling disease, and others not yet identified can become aquatic hitchhikers, and we all need to do our best to prevent their spread.

- Never put flies away wet or they will rust and get matted out of shape, and the dyes used in some fly-tying materials may run and spoil the colors of other flies in your box. Leave your fly box open on a sunny table or on the windshield of your car—but not exposed to the wind or you might return to a nearly empty box!

Midwinter Daydreams

92

How to keep your rod from breaking

MODERN GRAPHITE FLY RODS HAVE INCREDIBLE TENSILE strength, but the trend toward lighter rods has given us tools that don't have the crush strength of older graphite or fiberglass rods. You can land a 150-pound tarpon with a rod that weighs a few ounces, but that same rod won't survive even a glancing encounter with a ceiling fan or car door. To avoid breakage by fans and screen doors never put a fly rod together indoors. Never lean a rod against a car because the chances are good that it will either get slammed in a door or the wind will blow it over and someone will step on it. Always lean your rod up against a tree, rather than laying it flat on the ground, because those thin black tubes just disappear amongst the brush.

When transporting rods in a car or boat, resist the temptation to keep your rod strung up and banging around the deck of a boat or extending throughout the length of a compact car, bent against the windshield. We all do it, but you're just asking for trouble. If you want to transport your rod still strung with a leader and fly, use a rod-and-reel case that protects the rod during transit.

When stringing up a rod before fishing, don't pull the leader through the guides and then yank down on the leader to get the fly line out of the guides. Many rods are broken this way, and a better method is to pull the leader and some of the line straight out from the tip of the rod while the rod is placed on a safe, flat surface or held by another angler.

Many more rods are broken through carelessness when playing a fish, but one real danger area is when a fish is close to a boat, especially one that has sounded under the boat or at its side. Lifting straight up, with the rod tip in a near-vertical position, is a sure way to break a fly rod because the stress is concentrated at the fragile tip of the rod rather than using the more powerful butt. When a fish sounds near the boat, always try to play the fish at a sideways angle so you can use the lifting power of the boat. This may entail moving around the boat or asking the captain to back off a bit with the motor, but it will save you a broken rod.

Finally, be careful when using split shot or flies with heavily weighted eyes. Always try to cast a more open loop with these rigs and keep the weight away from yourself for safety reasons and from your rod for durability. A heavily weighted fly going well over a hundred miles per hour can frac-

ture the graphite if it hits the thin walls of a light fly rod. Even a glancing blow from a weighted fly can weaken a rod, resulting in a fracture on the next long cast or big fish. When investigating the "I was just casting and the rod suddenly broke" scenarios, the Orvis rod repair department inevitably finds that the angler was either fishing a Clouser Minnow or a big glob of split shot.

Trying to get the fly line out of the rod by pulling straight down on it is a fast track to a broken rod.

93

How to find leaks in your waders and how to patch them

YOUR WADERS WILL EVENTUALLY DEVELOP LEAKS. MOST leaks are easy to find and repair. The resulting patches give the waders character, and you'll avoid being tagged as a rookie. Of course, the surest way to find leaks is to fill the waders with water and see where it leaks out, but not only is this a major project and a major pain, the weight of all that water inside a pair of waders can put additional stress on the seams.

The first thing I try is to run a strong flashlight inside the suspected area in a dark room. Leaks show up as bright specks of light, and it's then easy to mark them with a marking pen. This works fine for wear spots and punctures, but seam leaks won't show up. For seam leaks, you can try holding the waders underwater in a bathtub and constricting the open part of the waders with hand pressure so you compress air against the seam. You can also try blowing up the waders with a shop vacuum that has a reversing feature. I've often used the vacuum-cleaner method after brushing the waders with a combination of dishwashing soap and water, because the leaks will show up as bubbles emanating from the seam.

Once you find a leak, clean the area with rubbing alcohol and let it dry. The best material for patching waders is special glue called Aquaseal that works on nylon, rubber, or polyester fabrics. For small punctures, seam leaks, or wear spots you simply brush some on and let it dry overnight. For large tears, you might have to apply the Aquaseal first, then slap a piece of old discarded wader fabric (many waders come with a piece of material for patching) over the tear, and then coat the surface of the patch, allowing some overlap. I've found that repairs using Aquaseal will outlast the rest of the wader, and I've never found glue that works as well.

You can patch your waders on the inside or the outside. The inside is neater and the patch is less subject to abrasion. But patching on the outside makes you look cool.

In the Canyon

X

Advanced

94

How to fish small dry flies

MOST FLY FISHERS REGARD FISHING SMALL DRY FLIES WITH the same enthusiasm as preparing income tax records. An enlightened minority relishes the opportunity because they know trout are less suspicious of artificial flies smaller than size 20, and since the fish have to eat a lot of the tiny stuff before getting full, there are more chances to fool them.

Don't let the thought of light tippets scare you away. Modern nylon and fluorocarbon tippets in 6X and 7X diameters are very strong, and can easily handle trout of twenty inches if you play the fish with a light touch. Small flies are more difficult to thread, but tying one on is not a major project as long as you are prepared with a pair of 4X or 5X reading glasses and/or a tool for threading small flies, of which there are dozens on the market.

These tiny flies are perfectly capable of hooking and holding large trout.

Seeing a small fly in the comfort of your own hands is not the same as seeing one fifty feet way in dim light. What most anglers don't realize is that even people who fish tiny flies all the time have just as much trouble as you do seeing a size 22 Griffith's Gnat on the water. They compensate by estimating where the fly is on the water, and when a fish rises anywhere near where they suspect their fly is drifting, they gently tighten up on the line. This seldom spooks a rising fish, and it takes very little pressure to set the hook with a small dry.

You can also fish a tiny fly as a dropper behind a bigger fly to help track its progress. Tie on a size 14 Parachute Adams, then tie a twenty-inch piece of 6X tippet to the bend of the bigger hook and the tiny fly of your choice on the end of this dropper. Or you can add a very tiny strike indicator or a piece of strike putty to your tippet—there is no law stating that strike indicators may only be used with nymphs.

Hooking fish with tiny flies is no problem, as penetration of the jaw is easy and once the hook is set it's very hard to dislodge it. You can take this on faith or you can stick a size 24 Blue Wing Olive into the tip of your thumb (similar to a trout jaw) and see how easy it is to dislodge.

95

Taking better fish pictures

WANT BETTER-LOOKING FISH PICTURES? KEEP YOUR FISH in the water. The color and movement of the water add drama and maintain the color of a fish better, plus it's better for catch-and-release fishing. And there is nothing more boring than a fish held at arms length out of the water in an unnatural pose, rather than half submerged in its environment. Whether it's a tiny jewel of a brook trout sparkling above the streambed or a giant tarpon held alongside a boat, I guarantee your pictures will be more interesting to you and your friends.

Prepare for the shot. Teach your fishing buddy or your guide how to use your camera before you start fishing. Make sure the camera is set on auto-focus and program or full-auto mode if someone unfamiliar with the camera is using it. And have them get the camera out well before you land the fish, discussing how you want the shot and planning the angle of the shot in relation to the sun and background as you are playing the fish.

You'll get more interesting pictures and release fish in a safer manner if you take photos of fish close to the water.

Set the zoom, if you have one, to as wide as possible so that you make sure to get the whole fish and yourself (if you want to be in the picture) in the frame. You can crop away unwanted background easily, but you can't create image data where it's missing without some serious Photoshop work. Besides, with your zoom set on wide angle, your depth of field will be deeper, ensuring that if the camera does not focus perfectly most everything in the image will still be sharp.

Fish are about as cooperative as four-year-old boys during photo sessions, and you'll need to freeze the action by using a fast shutter speed or flash. If your camera has manual settings or program shift, set it to a shutter speed of at least 1/250th of a second with natural light, or force the camera to flash by setting the flash to fire regardless of light conditions. Fill flash tends to make better fish pictures, even in bright light, because it freezes action and fills in shadows you may not notice in the excitement.

96

Spotting fish in the water

TROUT WON'T ALWAYS COOPERATE BY RISING AND bonefish won't always stick their fins or tails above the surface. In clear, shallow water, however, fly fishing to sighted fish is one of the most fascinating ways to catch them. Bright light and elevation always help in spotting fish. You usually can't do much about the amount of sunlight, and when fishing from a boat you already have some elevation, but you can often get just an incremental increase in height when wading or fishing from shore by backing up a bit, staying shallower than you might normally wade.

In bright sunlight, your best approach is to look for a fish's shadow. Fish are well camouflaged and reflect their background, but they present a solid block to sunlight and will cast a shadow that is nearly always more visible than the fish themselves. Also look for movement. Bonefish, striped bass, and redfish in shallow water are always moving, so if you are wading slowly and you think you've spotted a fish, stop for a moment, as it's more difficult to perceive movement in other objects when you are moving.

If you're fortunate, you'll see bonefish tailing in shallow water, where they are much easier to spot.

You will probably spot just a piece of a fish first and your brain will have to fill in the rest of the fish from memory. This is why people with more experience spotting fish are always better than those with less experience, even if the novice has sharper eyesight. A bonefish guide may only see the tail or a single fin of a bonefish, but the thousands of hours he's spent looking into the water help his brain make the connection quickly. You'll also learn to look for the unique colors of various fish, so you can automatically eliminate objects that don't fit into the right color scheme: bonefish are light gray/green, striped bass are gray/blue, redfish are a coppery color, brown trout are pale yellow/brown, and rainbow trout are blue/green.

Finally, polarized glasses are not just snake oil invented by a marketer. They truly remove glare from the water's surface, and those with an amber tint also enhance contrast in shallow water. Combined with a long-brimmed hat that keeps flare away from your sunglasses, polarized glasses won't make up for a lack of experience but they sure give you a jump start.

97

How to catch trout in the summer when the water is low and clear

TROUT ARE MORE DIFFICULT TO CATCH DURING LOW, clear summer flows, but this type of water can offer the most interesting fishing of the season. Fish will be spooky. Keep your profile low and your movements slow. Stay in the shade if possible, especially if you can keep your profile close to streamside brush, where your movements will be less noticeable. Wear drab olive or even camouflage clothing—lightweight cotton shirts made for dove hunting are perfect.

Summer means water temperatures that may reach the upper avoidance level for trout because warm water holds less of the life-giving oxygen they need than colder water. Look for fish in fast riffles or boulder-lined pocket water where the water gets more oxygen exchange, or fish below small

In the low-water conditions of summer and early fall, keep a low profile and wear drab clothing.

tributary streams or close to springs trickling off rocky banks. Trout will be more active in the morning than in the evening, because a trout stream is coldest just after dawn.

Unless grasshoppers are abundant, summer means tiny flies and light tippets. Most of the insects that hatch in the summer are small, and even the ants and beetles that fall into the water are seldom larger than a size 18, so stick with smaller flies and 6X or 7X tippets because not only will they look less suspicious, but tiny flies on light tippets land with less of a splash and won't spook wary trout. You may have to scale down on your fly rod as well. That 5- or 6-weight line that worked fine in June could make too much commotion in July and August.

Low and Clear

98

How to fish dry flies when nothing is rising

YOU DON'T HAVE TO WAIT FOR A HATCH TO FISH WITH dry flies. Although trout won't come to the surface under all conditions, there are certain times when you can fish a dry fly in a fishy-looking place even if you have not seen a fish rise all day. The fly pattern you use is not as critical as during a hatch, as long it is close in size and shape to something the fish eat on a regular basis. So if you see size-14 caddisflies clinging to brush along the riverbank, or if meadows surrounding a stream are full of grasshoppers, you have a pretty good idea of what fly pattern to use.

Riffled water is the best place to fish dry flies when nothing is rising.

The conditions that favor "blind fishing" a dry fly include:

- Water temperatures when trout are most active, between 55 and 65 degrees.
- Water less than two feet deep. Trout are reluctant to come to the surface when lying in deep water. Dry flies are deadly in small streams nearly all the time because the fish are never in deep water.
- Flow of one foot per second or less, about the speed of a slow walk. Trout have a tough time coming to the surface in fast current, but don't overlook pocket water with lots of rocks, because although the water looks fast, it holds many small eddies with slower current.
- Water with a slight chop. Gentle riffles are always better than flat water for blind fishing because the fish are less selective about what they eat and don't get as good an inspection of your fly.

99

How can you get started in fly tying?

IF YOU'RE INTERESTED IN TYING YOUR OWN FLIES, IT DOES require a commitment of time but little else. You don't have to have patience. (I've been tying flies for forty-five years and patience is not my strong suit.) You don't have to have tiny, nimble fingers. (The best tier of small dry flies I've ever known has fingers the size of bratwurst and drives an earth mover for a living.) You don't need superb eyesight. (Get plenty of light and a pair of 4X reading glasses and you'll do just fine.)

Begin by taking fly-tying classes if possible. Most fly shops offer them, and there is no substitute for someone looking over your shoulder as you tie. If you can't attend a class, buy a good basic fly-tying kit, one with a detailed book or manual. Make sure all the materials in the kit are labeled, as there is nothing more frustrating than reading instructions telling you to "tie in a six-inch piece of yellow chenille" when you don't know chenille

◀ *Fly Tying Legacy*

from hackle. A good kit will include a decent vise and materials. There is nothing more frustrating than a vise that won't hold a hook or a pair of scissors that doesn't cut cleanly. You can also get some great help from free videos on the Web, or from basic fly-tying DVDs. If you can't watch over someone's shoulder, a close-up video is the next best thing.

Start by tying Woolly Buggers and tie a dozen of them before moving on to something else. A Woolly Bugger teaches you many of the basic fly-tying skills—including applying a feather tail or wing, winding hackle, winding a body material, and whip finishing—in addition to the basic thread manipulation procedures. Besides, you can catch nearly any fish that swims on a Woolly Bugger, so your first efforts will begin to fill your fly box with an effective pattern.

100

Can you catch trout on a fly during the winter?

IT'S LEGAL TO FISH MANY TROUT STREAMS TWELVE months a year. Thus if you get addicted to fly fishing, there is no reason to suffer withdrawal or cabin fever just because it's January instead of June. Most of the best winter fishing is found in "tailwater" rivers or those influenced by stable releases from large dams. These rivers stay closer to optimum trout temperatures than runoff-influenced streams because most

With the right tackle and a little sun to warm the water, you can catch trout even in the dead of winter.

flow out of dams at about the temperature of ground water regardless of air temperature. Some of the best winter fisheries are in southern tailwaters like the Chattahoochee outside of Atlanta, the White and Red rivers in Arkansas, and the San Juan River in northern New Mexico. However, if you can wade through the snow to get to the river, all of the Rocky Mountain states have tailwater rivers with excellent winter fishing, such as the Bighorn and Madison rivers in Montana or the South Platte and Frying Pan in Colorado.

Winter fly fishing is mostly nymph fishing and dry-fly fishing with tiny midge imitations. Few mayflies, caddisflies, and stoneflies hatch during the winter, but midges will hatch on warmer days, especially during heavy cloud cover. Fish eating below the surface won't move far for a fly during the winter, either, so most of the fishing (save for the lucky circumstance of a midge hatch) is with a nymph, weight on the leader, and a strike indicator. Midge nymphs are the best flies in most rivers because midges are the only active aquatic insect.

Fish will usually be found in deeper, slower water, often in the middle of large pools. They seem to "pod up" in groups—I hesitate to use the word "school" because that implies a bunch of fish milling around in circles, while winter fish stayed glued to the bottom in most rivers. So if you catch one trout, chances are you'll find more of them close at hand.

101

A dozen fly-fishing books you should not be without

THE FOLLOWING DOZEN ARE THOSE FLY-FISHING technique reference books I would not be without. In addition, if you want if you enjoy the more literary side of fly fishing, read anything related to fly fishing by Jim Babb, Bill Barich, John Gierach, Jim Harrison, Ted Leeson, Nick Lyons, or Tom McGuane.

Brown, Dick. *Fly Fishing for Bonefish*. **Connecticut: The Lyons Press, 1993.** Bonefishing techniques from a master, with emphasis on Florida Keys and Bahamas techniques.

Weathered In

Caucci, Al, and Bob Nastasi. *Hatches II*. **New York: The Lyons Press, 1986.** There are hundreds of books on fishing hatches, but I keep coming back to this one for solid information.

Combs, Trey. *Steelhead Fly Fishing*. **Connecticut: The Lyons Press, 1991.** The bible of western steelhead fly fishers, from the sport's colorful history to tackle, fly selection, and fly presentation.

Deck, Tom. *The Orvis Fly-Casting Guide*. **Connecticut: The Lyons Press, 2003.** Based on the methods used by the Orvis Fly-Fishing Schools, the oldest and most comprehensive fly-fishing schools in the world.

Humphreys, Joe. *Joe Humphreys's Trout Tactics*. **Pennsylvania: Stackpole Books, 1989.** Great insight on small stream fishing and nymphing by a master of fly presentation.

Kaufmann, Randall. *Bonefishing with a Fly*. **Oregon: Frank Amato Publications, 1992.** A great overview of bonefishing, with excellent diagrams and text on the life cycle of the bonefish and life on the flats.

Kreh, Lefty and Mark Sosin. *Practical Fishing Knots*. **Connecticut: The Lyons Press, 1991.** Pretty much the bible on knots for fly fishing as well as conventional fishing knots.

Krieger, Mel. *The Essence of Fly Casting*. **San Francisco: Club Pacific, 1987.** A complete guide to learning to cast, improving your cast, and identifying problems, by one of the most talented and generous mentors in fly casting.

LaFontaine, Gary. *Caddisflies*. **Connecticut: The Lyons Press, 1994.** Caddisflies are more important than mayflies in many rivers, and if you want to learn more about their habits, this is the bible.

Rosenbauer, Tom. *Prospecting for Trout*. **Connecticut: The Lyons Press, 2000.** You don't always see hatches on a trout stream, and this book helps you understand the techniques used to catch trout when they aren't rising.

Supinski, Matt. *Steelhead Dreams*. **Oregon: Frank Amato Publications, 2001.** Great Lakes steelhead biology and life cycles, fishing all four seasons, fly selection, playing and landing fish, and much more from one of the most experienced Great Lakes steelhead guides.

Tapply, Bill. *The Orvis Pocket Guide to Fly Fishing for Bass*. **Connecticut: The Lyons Press, 2003.** Fly-rod bass fishing is not that technical, and this complete little pocket guide tells you all you need to know.